EX LIBRIS

The Grace of Being There

SINGLE MOTHER SAINTS IN OUR LIVES

Edited by Summer Kinard

Written by:
Charlotte Riggle
Sandra C. Anderson
Elissa Bjeletich Davis
Elizabeth Gatling
Kristina Roth
Carrie Chuff
Angela Doll

Illustrated by Mary Sarchizian

PARK END BOOKS

Sugar Land, Texas
2022

Cover art & Illustrations: Mary Sarchizian
Cover art & illustrations Copyright © Mary Sarchizian

Publisher's Cataloging-in-Publication Data

Names: Kinard, Summer, 1977- editor.
Title: The Grace of Being There: single mother saints in our lives / edited by Summer Kinard; illustrations by Mary Sarchizian
Description: Sugar Land [Texas]: Park End Books, 2022.
Identifiers: ISBN: 978-1-953427-24-3
Subjects: Religion - Christian Living - Family & Relationships, Religion - Christian Living - Women's Interests, Religion - Christianity - Saints & Sainthood

www.parkendbooks.com

From Sandra Anderson:
Thankful and forever grateful to God for my daughter Nicole, who encouraged me to share my truth so that we could continue our healing, and for my dearest sister in Christ Melpo, who gently convinced the 'talker' to write.

From Elizabeth Gatling:
For Gabriel who made me a mom
For Mom who taught me how to be a mom
For Suggie who taught her how to be a mom
For all my "Other Mothers" who continued to teach me
For Saint Anthousa who gives me hope
For Saint Ruth who reminded me that I am "a worthy woman"

From Charlotte Riggle:
With love and gratitude to Corinne, Susan, Sarah, Fran, and Margaret, whose steadfast love and kindness sustained me and my children while I was a single mom.

From Elissa Bjeletich Davis:
With deep gratitude to Carol and Whitney, who listened patiently for countless hours, crying and laughing with me through the dark years of my divorce. Their love and prayers sustained me.

From Kristina Roth:
To my amazing boy, and to women everywhere raising children on your own.

From Mary Sarchizian:
For the people who helped me walk when I was too afraid to move.

From Carrie Chuff:
To my mother, who showed me what it means to be courageous, persevering, and have a spirit of true generosity and love.

From Summer Kinard:
For all the mother saints who kiss our foreheads while we sleep.

From Angela Doll:
Dedicated to my children, who made this heart a mother's heart.

Table of Contents

Introduction:

MERCY ALWAYS, ANYWAY

I OPENED MY EYES on people who loved me. In the furthest reaches of my memory, I can hear the music of their voices, the laughter warm enough to ripen fruit. I see the swirl of faces of my uncles and aunts and my grandmother and great-grandparents and great-aunts, people who took me onto their knees and dandled me, the little foundling child, giving me not quite a place at the table, but a place in the arms of everyone at it. I grew up with people who loved me, but not with my father. By the time I was born, my father had already taken himself out of the picture for most of my life. He wasn't the sort of man to be proud of. He was older than my mother and used her, siring me on my mother's seventeenth (read: *legal*) birthday, abandoning us both four months before I was born. I inherited his musical ability and hazel eyes but nothing else. My mother got plenty, though. She got kicked out of high school, given a set of lewd nicknames, and a couple of decades of malicious whispers from people who considered themselves better than her. I grew up with people who loved her, loved me, *anyway*.

There was another young woman around 1,500 years ago whose story could have been one of shame. St. Non was a young Welsh woman who was raped by a local king and became pregnant with a son who grew to be St. Dewi (David), the patron saint of Wales. Her birth-giving was so painful that her fingerprints marked a stone she was holding, and lightning struck the stone in two when the child was finally born. Later the split stone became the foundation under the Altar of a church, the very emblem of God breaking stones asunder and giving life from the hardest parts of our existence. St. Non refused to be ashamed of her son, refused to be married off in order to be silenced, and lived a life of such holiness and prayer that both she and her son became saints. After her death in a convent, at least three pilgrimage sites were dedicated to St. Non, and her prayers work toward the healing of the many victims of sexual violence who reach out to her. She was fierce enough to mark a stone with her suffering, and God who split that stone in two gave steady grace so that she and her son became two cornerstones of the Celtic Church. St. Non didn't love *anyway*. She loved steadily, the way God loves.

Being loved *anyway* isn't the same as being loved outright. When I was introduced at family gatherings, there were calculations in the grownups' eyes. I would see the moment they finished their long division, the lift of the brow when they recognized me as the remainder of a tricky equation. The way they treated me once they'd done the math told me what kind of person they were. The good ones—my mother's huge Catholic family, my stepfather's Pentecostal relatives, the librarians at my grandmother's job, the preacher and Sunday school teacher at my step-grandmother's Baptist church— would love me *anyway* the way you love the scraps from sugar cookies after you've cut out the planned shapes. I could tell they still believed in my basic sweetness and potential, even if some of them doubted I'd turn out without lumps.

The other kind of calculator didn't love me *anyway*. Those people might be kind in their own way, but it was the kindness they would give to a pauper or a servant. They made sure to preserve the distinction of rank. When I went to their houses, I was invited to play with the dog toys. I was told to stay in the kitchen while they whispered viciously about my mother and called her names that I didn't understand but knew would get my mouth washed out with soap if *I* said them. When that family gathered for holidays, the other grandchildren received ten times the presents. When that family shopped for clothes for a photograph, the other granddaughters were bought cute outfits from a department store, while I was bought an ill-fitting tank top and short shorts from a rushed thrift store stop, because "my mother was poor."

There's nothing in the law of God or the Gospel of Jesus Christ that tells people to shame single mothers or their children. In fact, the steady covenant love of God in the Old and New Testaments sets out quite the opposite pattern: God doesn't scorn or abandon people broken off the core of community. Rather, He restores, defends, and calls them by His name. Having a father give you his name makes a difference in how people in the world size you up, but having The Father call you by name and give you His Name reaches so much further. That God, that Father, does not abandon mothers. That God, that Father, does not forsake children. His love is steady, like St. Non's, like St. Anthousa's, like St. Helena's, like the love experienced and lived by all of the women in this book, whether their children became well-known saints or not. That God loves us not *anyway* but *always*.

I had thought that people would have figured that out by now. I had noticed in my reading over the years that a lot of big-name saints were reared by single parents: St. Brigid, St. David of Wales, St. Mammas, St. Barbara (though her ultimately violent, authoritarian father was not a holy example!), the children of some of the saints in this book (Sts. Faith, Hope, and Love, St. Constantine the Great, St. John Chrysostom, St. Augustine of Hippo), and others. I thought that there must be some resource on how these saints reached out to faithful Christians who found themselves facing an unexpected path of parenting. Yet, when I went looking for resources for a single parent friend, I was disappointed to find that there was not even one Orthodox or Catholic book on single parent saints. I asked some of my friends to remedy that lack. Except for Carrie Chuff and I, who were reared by single mothers but who are not single mothers ourselves, the authors of this book have spent some part of their motherhood as single parents. They have each experienced the steady love of God through keeping company with the saints. Their stories bear witness to the truth that every type of family can be the good ground that nurtures the seeds of Christ's Kingdom.

You will find here the stories of five saints venerated in both the Orthodox and Catholic Churches, plus one Orthodox and one Catholic saint. These are not the saint stories you can find in synaxaria or on the internet or in children's books, though I hope you will look them up. Rather, I asked the authors to show the fruits of life with these saints. In order to encourage women who face single parenting, it's not enough to give them a distant example of a paper doll saint. I wanted readers to see in living stories how the living saints share with us the steady love and energy of the living God. Christ is the root of the saints' lives and our lives. In these pages you will see the fruit of those lives, woven together, so that you come to know the saints through the lives of Christians struggling alongside you now, in contexts you will recognize. I want you to see that you and your children are tucked alongside these saints and these writers under the Virgin Mary's cloak. I want you to see that you are embodying God the Father's grace by being there for your children. It is my prayer that, by the intercession of these saints and Our Holy Mother Mary, you will be strengthened and built up, encouraged, and restored to your place at the Father's table as one who is loved *always*.

In Christ,
Summer Kinard
Senior Editor and Owner, Park End Books
St. Non's Day 2022

Courageous Hospitality

THE WIDOW OF ZAREPHATH

I KINGS 17: 7-16

Charlotte Riggle

WHEN YOU'RE A SINGLE MOM, hospitality can feel impossible. How can you offer hospitality when, after work every day, day after day, you pick up the baby from daycare, and the older kids from their after-school program, get everyone home, put supper on, feed the baby, have supper with the kids, get one or two of them bathed, read bedtime stories, say prayers, and put them to bed, and collapse into a heap? When is there time for hospitality, when you need to do laundry and buy groceries and schedule a checkup for the baby and one of the kids needs posterboard and markers and a trip to the library for a poster project that's due by Tuesday?

But maybe it feels so impossible because you're thinking of hospitality the wrong way. At least, I was. Hospitality, in my mind, was sparkling conversation and delicious food and an immaculately clean house. I couldn't manage any of that.

In the Scriptures, though, the word that gets translated into English as hospitality is philoxenia, the love of strangers, of foreigners, of people who aren't like you. Offering hospitality isn't inviting your friends over for dinner. It's being kind to someone you don't even know. And the kindness doesn't mean a lavish meal in a spotless house. Hospitality is as simple as offering a cup of cold water to someone who is thirsty.

Abraham's servant asked Rachel for a little water from her pitcher. Jesus asked Photini for a drink. And before he asked her for bread, Elijah asked the widow of Zarephath for a cup of water.

The widow of Zarephath. There is so much we don't know about her. We don't know how long she and her husband had been married. Maybe they had been married for many years, and had many children, and she was pregnant when a plague came and took the rest of her family. After all that loss, all that pain, she had delivered a son, a precious boy. That baby boy was the reason she could go on living.

Or maybe she and her husband had been married only a year or two, and they were so happy when their first child, their son, was born. They smiled and cooed and talked about how much he looked like his father. Then her husband, the father of her child, was injured, and the wound festered, and there was nothing that anyone could do for him, nothing that she could do, while he waited to die.

Maybe her husband left her well provided for when he died, or maybe they had little to start with, and when he died, that little crumbled to dust and was gone.

We don't know any of that. We don't even know her name.

All we know is that she was a single mom, and she was desperately poor.

Maybe there's a reason that the Holy Spirit didn't tell us any more about her than that. Because all of us who are or have been single moms can see our lives in hers. She is one of us. We are her.

Before the drought, neighbors may have provided for the widow of Zarephath and her son. But as the drought went on, and the rains refused to fall, people's hearts closed against her. They had to take care of their own families. They had nothing to offer her or her son.

Or perhaps she never asked for their help. Perhaps she didn't want to be a burden. Perhaps she wanted to prove to someone, to her neighbors, to herself, that she could manage on her own.

Or perhaps she was like me. Perhaps, when she found herself a single mother, she felt lost and alone and unable to manage the life that had suddenly become her life, a life she had never wanted or expected. Perhaps she felt an overwhelming need for the support of her community, her friends and neighbors, and at the same time felt ashamed for wanting that support.

Perhaps all the work involved in being a single mom meant that she didn't have the space or the time to work out how she felt. When the loss and shame and neediness and pain overpowered her, she stuffed the feelings down into her stomach, like I did, where she could ignore them while she did what she had to do, one day at a time, one hour at a time, one breath at a time.

And the drought went on. The widow of Zarephath made what little she had last as long as she could, and she made sure her son ate even if there was nothing for her. For a while, she was hungry all the time, but she had eaten so little for so long that the hunger had passed.

Then the day came that she knew would come. She had nothing but a bit of oil in a jug, and a handful of flour. With a small fire and a bit of water, she could make a small loaf of flat bread to share with her son, a last meal before they died.

God had told her that a man would come to Zarephath and ask her for food, and she should feed him. But it would be too late when the man of God arrived. She would have nothing to give.

She stood up wearily and made her way to the city gate. She didn't have the strength to go further, but the gate was far enough. She needed only a couple of sticks to cook the small loaf she would make. Once they had eaten, she thought, she would lie down with her son in her arms and hold him and comfort him until his breathing stopped, just as she had comforted his father, her husband, as he took his last breaths. And then, alone, she would die.

While she was gathering sticks, a stranger, a foreigner, a man she'd never met, approached her cautiously. Had the man of God come after all?

The man looked at her. He had not eaten as well recently as he was accustomed to eating, but the ravens had fed him well enough. He didn't understand why God would send him to this city, the home of his adversary, to ask a widow for food. Especially not this widow. Her face was gaunt, her hands skeletal. How could she feed him, when she clearly had nothing?

The widow watched him silently, until the man broke the silence. "I am thirsty. Can you bring me a cup water?"

He was only a thirsty traveler, then, she thought, and not the man of God. She nodded and turned to get water for him. And then he called after her. "Can you bring me a bit of bread as well?"

So, it was him. It was the man, the one God had told her was coming to ask her for food. God had told her to give him food. But how could she? How could she give him her son's bread?

She didn't have the strength to be angry, not at this man, and not at his God. The only defense she had was truth. So, she threw the truth at him. "I have no bread," she said. "I have a handful of flour, and a few drops of oil. As you can see, I've gathered two sticks, and I'm going to go home, and make my son some bread, and we will eat it, and then we will die."

Her truth cut Elijah. Suddenly, his heart was filled with compassion for this woman, and with the compassion came anger. How could God make him the instrument of this woman's death? He took his anger, and wrapped her truth in it, and threw it at God. In an instant, he understood that God wouldn't let her food run out. That's why God had sent him to Zarephath. He was there because God loved this woman, this widow. He was there to make sure that she wouldn't die in this terrible drought, this drought that he himself had created. God wouldn't let him be the cause of her death. God wouldn't let her food run out. God wouldn't let her die.

So, he told her to do as she had planned. "But make me a bit of bread first, before you make the bread for yourself and your son. Because the Lord, the God of Israel, has promised me that your food won't run out until the rains return."

Did the widow of Zarephath believe that his God could multiply her food? Did it matter? If she didn't bring him food, she and her son would soon be dead anyway. If she brought him food, perhaps his God would honor his promise, and they wouldn't die. In any case, she had never in her life failed in her duty to offer hospitality to strangers. She would fulfill this duty once more, and then she would die.

She did as the stranger asked and brought him food. For this, St. Ephraim the Syrian called her a woman of faith, a woman of obedience. And she truly was those things. The midrash, though, the ancient rabbinical writings, called her a woman of valor, of courage, because she stretched out her hand to the needy.

When you are facing your own loss and your own fears, when your own needs overwhelm you, hospitality requires courage.

How did the widow of Zarephath find the courage to invite Elijah into her home? Bringing bread to him where he stood in the city gate is one thing. Bringing him to her home, where she and her son were alone and vulnerable, seems like another thing entirely.

My house was on the dividing line between residential and commercial. From our front door, we saw our neighbors' homes, tucked under large, leafy trees. Looking out the back, we saw the drive through at the Taco Bell.

At the end of the month, people who had run out of food, and didn't have enough money even for a meal at Taco Bell, would sometimes ring the bell at my front door. I'd answer, and see a stranger standing there. Always men. Ever so politely, they'd ask if I could give them money so they could buy food.

I was afraid. I lived there, alone with my children, and I didn't want strange men thinking I had money in the house. So, I didn't give them money. I'd go to the kitchen, and get a grocery bag, and fill it up, and bring it to the stranger at the door. That felt safer than giving them money.

One day, the man at the door seemed particularly young. His face was both handsome and hopeful. He told me that he was out of money, and his baby needed milk, and could I help him? Of course, I could. I had just gotten milk that morning, and I had 2 unopened cartons in the fridge. I brought him the milk, and opened the door to hand it to him, and his face fell. I thought for a moment that he would cry.

"My baby drinks Similac," he said.

My baby drank Enfamil, not Similac. "Wait a moment," I said. I put the milk back in the fridge, and found my purse, and opened my wallet. I had a $20 and some change. I put the money in the man's hands. "I hope this is enough," I said. "It's all I have right now."

It was a far cry from the hospitality the widow offered Elijah. But it was all that I had the courage to do.

As small as it was, it took courage for me to offer the hospitality the young man needed. It took so much more courage for him to ask for the help he needed. Hospitality is that way. Philoxenia isn't a one-way street. The word applies to both the one who gives and the one who receives. It takes courage to offer, and courage to ask. So much courage.

Asking for help makes you vulnerable. The person you ask might refuse you, might scorn you, might shame you. Even if they do nothing to shame you, you might well shame yourself, because you have to ask. We're all brought up to think we should be independent, that we must take care of ourselves and our own, and not rely on the charity of strangers. At least, that was true for me.

And yet, it seems that God wants us to depend on the charity of strangers. He told the widow of Zarephath to feed Elijah, and he told Elijah to feed the widow. They had to receive hospitality from each other to survive.

Why then, was it so hard for me to ask for help? I had four kids. I couldn't be in four places at once. I had to ask for help. Sometimes, it was as simple and easy as asking another mom to give one of the kids a ride to their soccer game, because otherwise the baby wouldn't get a nap. That felt okay. But how do you ask someone to help you clean your house, because every last plate or glass you own is in the sink or on the counter, and the laundry has piled up, and you are exhausted and overwhelmed and can't figure out what to do?

I didn't have the strength to ask. I was ashamed of the mess.

As it turned out, I didn't have to ask. Like the widow of Zarephath, I just had to be willing to accept what was offered.

It was easier for me. The offer didn't come from a strange man. It came from a woman I knew well, a friend. She came to my house, and asked me whether I'd rather she clean my kitchen or fold the pile of clean laundry? So, we talked while she cleaned the kitchen and I sat and folded laundry. That was such an unimaginable gift. It wasn't a gift that made the difference between living and dying. But it made a difference in my heart. It made me feel less broken, and more whole.

Philoxenia always has that effect. It doesn't just feed the hungry and clothe the naked and shelter the homeless. It does all that, of course. But it does more. It softens hearts. It nurtures compassion. It grows mercy. It heals.

That's why God sent Elijah to the widow. He wanted to teach Elijah compassion.

Elijah had decided to prove God's power, and punish Ahab, by stopping the rain. And then he went and hid in a valley. He hid himself from the suffering that he had caused. God had pity on him, and sent him food, and waited. But Elijah's heart was full of the need to prove that everything he believed about God was true, and the need to punish sinners. His heart held no mercy, no compassion for the innocent people who were suffering in his drought.

God saw the suffering, though, and he wanted Elijah to see it, too. So, he sent Elijah to the widow.

Elijah had compassion on the widow. He fed her, and her son. But his compassion didn't extend to anyone else. He still kept the sky closed. He still kept the rain from falling.

God gave him time at the widow's house, just as he had given him time in the valley. He waited. As he waited, more people suffered, and more people died. And Elijah wouldn't give up his drought to save anyone's life.

Until the widow's son died.

I don't know if Elijah had ever told the widow that he had brought on the drought, and that he had the power to bring it to an end. Somehow, I don't think he did. I don't think the widow ever knew.

But even if she didn't know that Elijah was responsible for the never-ending drought, when her son died, she knew Elijah was responsible for that. She told him so: "What do you have against me, man of God? Did you come to remind me of my sin and kill my son?"

Her truth cut Elijah's heart once again. The accusation hurt enough that he accepted the responsibility that she threw at him. He knew that he had caused her son's death. He had caused her suffering. He also understood that when he had taken her last morsel of food, he had become responsible for her wellbeing. Her accusation filled him, not yet with compassion, but with shame.

He took her son's lifeless body to his room, and cried out to God: "Have you brought tragedy even on this widow I am staying with, by causing her son to die?"

Asking God to feed the widow and her son was one thing. He knew that God could provide bread as long as it was needed. He had done it for the Israelites in the wilderness. He could do it for the widow and her son. But asking him to give the boy back his life was a different thing entirely. Never in the history of the world had God done anything like that. Elijah knew that. And yet Elijah demanded that God remove his shame and give the boy back his life.

God answered his cry. In the Jewish tradition, God told Elijah that he could hold the key to the rains, or he could hold the key to life, but he couldn't hold both. If he wanted the boy to live, he had to give up the drought.

Elijah looked into his heart, and it was filled with compassion. He realized that, more than he wanted to punish Ahab, more than he wanted to prove God's power, he wanted this boy to live.

You never know what will come of the hospitality that you offer, or the hospitality that you receive. If you knew, it wouldn't take courage. The only thing the widow of Zarephath knew for sure was that God had called her to offer hospitality one last time before she and her son died. In doing that, she showed us how to give even when we think we have nothing left to give. And in giving, the widow received her life, and the life of her son.

REFLECTION QUESTIONS

1) Where in your household do you need help? Who might you ask to help you?

2) When have you experienced someone showing you compassion?

3) How can you show compassion to yourself, your child[ren], and people in your community?

4) Shame can keep us from asking for help, or it can motivate us to notice injustice and needs, the way it did for Elijah. Where do you feel shame? Can you ask God to help you change something so that you participate in healing instead?

All in With Christ

SAINT PHOTINI
JOHN 4: 5-42

Sandra C. Anderson

"I have not come to call the righteous, but sinners to repentance"
Luke 5:32

I WANT TO WEAVE a tapestry for you to show you how my life was saved by the grace and mercy of God, just like St. Photini. How can you liken yourself to a saint? Well, you can't, but these two threads of my life and Saint Photini's life are both woven by the grace of God. It's that grace that I want to show you. Keep in mind tapestries are beautiful on front and quite a mess in the back. Yet, the image is still beautiful, especially when it depicts the truth.

Let me take a moment to thread my loom with a comparison. Photini was transformed after a twenty-minute conversation as she stood face to face with Christ. It took more like twenty years for me to acquire my new life in Him. She had an experience that started a million stories; my encounter with Christ is a long story. My weaving thread has three strands: Christ, Photini, and me. I am the weakest of the three, but a cord with three strands cannot be easily broken. My story has a pattern now because of the strength with which those two held me. The pattern is this: I never did anything that God didn't forgive and redirect toward the good He meant for me and the people in my life. I failed miserably at my endeavors. I was sometimes a crappy mom. I almost tore this tapestry to pieces. Yet He could and did repair those things when I asked Him. This required life-renewing work on my part. As you read my story, I want you to remember that with God all things are possible.

In the spirit of truth (pun intended), I was a terrible single mom: young, selfish, unprepared in every way. I was a broken person. Broken people love, but their love and good intentions often slip through the cracks of brokenness and do not fully reach their intended. To go back to the weaving metaphor, I missed a LOT of stitches. Right here I would love to give you all kinds of excuses and self-justify the things that I did. The bottom line is, I made bad decisions over and over. Certainly, I made those decisions due to the circumstances of my life at the time. Still, I knew right from wrong, and I still made the wrong choices anyway. I made most of these bad choices when I had no faith and believed I alone was in charge of my life.

Photini knew right from wrong, as well. Her bad choices caused her to go from man to man (husband or not) in order to survive. It's hard to maintain your self-worth or self-esteem when you can't seem to maintain a loving relationship. How many times was she hurt or disappointed? With each new man did she keep hoping, "Please let this man be the one to truly love and stay with me"? It seems Photini's 'well' was bad relationships.

Though she felt ashamed, it didn't stop how she was living, just as my shame didn't stop me. Difference is, you can bet I did way worse than Photini could have ever dreamed of.

I buried my shame with drugs and alcohol, because I was too weak to stop what I was doing or trust that I could do better if I had just believed in myself. Instead, I listened, acted, and lived up to the low expectations people had for me. Somehow, I managed to keep all my jobs and a roof over our heads. In hindsight I know now this was by the grace of God and not so much my doing.

I have a litany of sins I could write about, but this is not a novel; it is a few pages. Here are the shadows in the background of my redemption: I stole, I drank, did drugs, I had an abortion, and I slept with men. Although no money was left on the nightstand, so to speak, make no mistake: there were transactions. I was surviving, not living.

I ask your indulgence here as I explain a bit of my life growing up. Something relevant to my story—not an excuse, mind you—bears sharing. I was illegitimate. This was a big deal in 1949. It came complete with the right amount of shame and lies that I had to keep and tell. I wasn't event baptized till I was 10 years old, and that was only after a family friend shamed my mother into it.

As a child, I lived much of the time with my kind, faithful, and very loving grandmother. The Greek Orthodox Church was her second home. As a result, I spent a lot of time there, as well. I was with her as she helped with cleaning, dropped off kolivas, baked prosforo, and repaired vestments and various other altar linens. I knew when to stand, kneel, and do my cross. The Liturgy was all in Greek, so I mimicked. Don't get me wrong: I loved being in church. I loved the smell, the icons, sitting up close so I could see the designs on the fabric of father's vestments. I sang in the choir. I didn't know what I was singing, but I stayed on key. Mostly, I loved sitting next to my grandmother. I knew never to cross my legs, lest I feel the vise grip of my tiny grandmother's hand on my knee. (Let us be attentive!) I learned to love church from my grandmother, and I saw that she loved 'O Theos' with all her heart. Unfortunately for me, everything I loved had nothing to do with a personal relationship with God. I didn't learn anything about the faith. That's what it was like for me as a Cradle. It was assumed that the relationship would happen by osmosis, I guess.

Fast forward. It's was 1992. I'd remarried. My daughter was a teenager, and much damage had been done to our relationship. Basically, she hated me. (I wasn't surprised.) My husband and I were drowning in our secular life, and we couldn't seem to find a lifeline.

One Sunday morning, on our third pot of coffee for fighting off hangovers, I had an epiphany. My husband and I were both raised with faith in our lives. Albeit mine was not as regular as his, still it was a part of both of our lives in the past, and we had abandoned it for many years. We were on the brink of a possible divorce. Since everything we were doing to change our circumstances was not working, we decided that we should investigate finding a church, to possibly reconnect to our base.

We went a few churches, but neither of us felt any connection. After a few unsuccessful tries, I remembered thinking that there was a Greek church relatively nearby. We thought, "Okay. Let's try it." (On a side note: I can't stress this enough. Thank God the liturgy was in English, or all the transformation that happened after our visit would never have happened! We would not have understood anything should it have been in Greek.)

They say that, "A life of sin can be changed with one good decision." The woman at the well made the greatest good decision of her life. She heard the good news, she believed, and she decided to share it with the world!

Jesus told her not to bother about where to worship. He explained to her that the time had come for everyone to worship the right way: to worship the Father in spirit and in truth. He told her the Father is looking for those who worship in this way. He told her God is spirit. He explained that it's not the physical place we worship that is important. It's that we worship in our hearts and minds, the truth of our belief in him.

That was a lot to process for anyone, right? She was waiting on the Messiah who was going to come and explain all things, and there was Jesus telling her not to bother waiting–He was already there. "I am He." Who did our Lord see fit to receive this bombshell of truth? Not a rabbi, not a Pharisee, ... heck, not even a man! Nope, it was the simple, sinful "woman at the well."

On Pentecost, this woman was baptized along with her five sisters and two sons. She was given the name Photini, meaning the "Enlightened One." She and her family traveled as missionaries all through Samaria and into Africa for over thirty years. The family then went to Rome, where they were eventually martyred by Emperor

Nero during his persecution of Christians. Ironically, Photini was thrown into a dry well, where she was heard praising, singing and proclaiming Christ the Risen Lord! It should be noted that all of her family became Saints and endured Martyrdom.

Back to our one good decision when we returned to church that Sunday. Well, I don't want to sound like some big bible-thumping revival preacher, but Hallelujah! Boy, did we find Jesus! (I won't speak more about my husband. Although we took this first step together, this writing is about my spiritual journey. His journey is not my story to tell.)

When I walked into the Narthex and lit my candle, I immediately seemed to be on autopilot. It felt so natural to take the candle, do my cross, and of course, fish in my purse for a dollar bill! It is impossible to describe what happened to me when I walked into the sanctuary.

It was like I had been falling down a deep hole, frightened by what would be waiting for me at the bottom. Yet, when I sat down and took a breath, I felt that I had landed on a soft cloud that encompassed my whole body. It wasn't a hole after all, but a well. Everything came rushing back to me: the smells, the sounds, the sights, the warmth and comfort of the saints surrounding me.

The old joke is: *How many Orthodox does it take to change a lightbulb? None. We never change.* Thank God for this most beautiful gift of the consistency in the faith. It allows me to always feel at home whenever or wherever I step inside the 'heaven on earth' that is the church. Even though I felt the presence of Christ in the church, my transformation was gradual, unlike Photini's. I went to church faithfully for a couple years and fully engaged in all the ministries. I had always loved serving others, especially the elderly. My grandmother had used to take me to visit all the old people all the time. I laughed remembering that, because she called *them* old, when to me she seemed ancient. Doing for others had been a huge part of her life, and I didn't realize as a child that serving others had been her answer to Christ's calling. Yet her strong excellent example stayed with me all my life, even in the worst of times. It was her example that I followed as I began to weave beauty back into my life.

It was not until after going on a pilgrimage to the Holy Land that I realized I had only put my toes in the water. I had not really immersed myself in the faith. All the monasteries and churches dedicated to the saints and apostles told the story of their confession and repentance and transformations in Christ. I HAD NOT GONE TO CONFESSION. This was the thing I knew I had to do, but I was terrified for anyone to find out the truth about me. I had picked myself up moved away from everyone who knew me, and I could pretend to be whoever I wanted. I could rewrite my story instead of owning it. That's what I had done. I thought that by doing all the things I was doing, that it would be enough. I could become who I was pretending to be.

I was baptized, so I took Communion. I had no idea what a transgression that was until I got home from my trip and realized I never should have partaken in the Eucharist until I had gone to confession. I honestly never knew anyone in my family who ever went to confession. I'm sure my grandmother must have, but she didn't share that with me.

How could I even tell a woman friend from church that I was a terrible mother, a party girl, and that I'd slept with more men than St. Mary of Egypt (if that's possible)? I couldn't do that! Then, how would I ever tell my priest? Would he still let me near the kids? Would he think different of me, or worse, would he be ashamed of me, like so many before him?

Photini stood before Christ and said, "I have no husband." That was confession. Jesus never really asked her to confess. She instinctively told the truth. Well, that's all fine and dandy, but I had way more to confess than having had a live-in boyfriend. The thought of confession was overwhelming. I was scared to death that I might lose all the good I had gained in my life since entering the church that day. I didn't understand that confession was a gift, not a punishment.

I stopped the priest one day in church and asked if I could go to confession. He asked me when I had gone last, and I told him, "Ah...Never?" Needless to say, he was shocked. I thought he would walk me over to where I'd seen him sit with others in confession, but instead he said, "I think you should call the office and schedule an appointment." Well, having to time to think about it was killing me. I was losing my resolve.

I spoke to a friend who was also a priest and told him my dilemma. He was so kind and said, "You don't have to tell him how many men you slept with, how many drugs you did, or how often, etc., just that you did these things." That advice eased my mind and probably saved Father and I about two hours of time. I wouldn't have to name how many "husbands" I had had. The Lord would know.

When Photini told Jesus her truth, Jesus just sat with her and continued their conversation. No loud voice shouted out of the sky, "SINNER! WHORE!" Their conversation made a cover for my shame, a little place aside where I could reveal myself without fear of being smitten by divine judgment. The minute I opened my mouth to speak, no words would come, only tears. I could not stop crying. Father waited so patiently till I could catch my breath. Once the words came, it was like a fountain overflowing, with my words spilling out all over the altar in front of the icon of Christ.

When Father put the stole on my head and said the prayer, *"May our Lord and God, Jesus Christ, by the grace and compassion of His love for mankind, forgive you, MY CHILD, all your transgressions. And I His unworthy Priest, through the power given me, forgive and absolve you from all your sins,"* it was the first time in my life I truly felt like a child of God. I still feel this restored relationship every time I go to confession. (I am happy to say, these days my confessions are a lot shorter than the first one.) I still need to go, and I still feel blessed to be able to.

Unfortunately, not all of us have been blessed with loving earthly parents. Because of this, many of us struggle just a little more in life. It is not an excuse, but it is a reality. Without the example of Godly parents, some of us take longer to get where we need to go, back into the Father's house, back into our place as His children.

Christ had always been with me, but I had to knock down the walls of sin I had built around my heart. I had always wondered why it was that I did not die of an overdose, gotten arrested for drugs or theft, lived through cancer, and why when I was at my bottom, I sought Him out. That was no random thought I had that morning with the coffee. It was all Him. God gives us free will. I had misunderstood mine. I had thought my free will meant I ought to do whatever I wanted, to choose anything that appealed in the moment. I did not realize that what I was in charge of was choosing God or not. When I finally chose Him, my whole life changed.

My priest did not admonish me. He loved me and helped guide me to live a healthier, stronger faith life. He encouraged me to learn more about our faith, to attend more services and retreats.

Christ told Photini we would all begin to worship in the Spirit of Truth. Both of us told our truths, repented, and received the Holy Spirit into our hearts and minds. Photini went on to be a great Evangelizer, believing in Christ and sharing the truth of his Resurrection. I think of her being the gold thread that runs through a tapestry, each stitch another person she brought to Christ, weaving us together as one in Him.

I did not become a great Evangelizer, and certainly not a Saint. But I did drink the Water, and my life changed forever. I was blessed to become a new person in Christ, to live a full life of Joy. I was able to work for the church for seventeen years, building new ministries and creating ways for others to serve for the Glory of God.

Because of the changes in me, I was able to repair my relationship with my daughter. God gave me the opportunity to be her mother again. No matter how old we are, we still need our mothers. By His grace, she still wanted one. Me.

Just as I had attained a new knowledge of a Heavenly Father, I also got to know and love my Heavenly Mother. By her example, I was able to listen to my daughter, to hear her pain, to ask her forgiveness and not let my pride (that urge to justify my actions) get in the way of healing. This transformation, the reconciliation with my daughter, and my marriage of thirty-five years to my faithful, God-loving husband, are among my greatest gifts. (Taste and See that the Lord is Good.)

God has woven grace into my complicated life, and in His light, I have become a faithful witness. When I stand to sponsor a child for baptism, I mean every word I say. When I tell my daughter that I love her, I mean it. When I see Christ face to face, He will know that I mean it with every fiber of my being when I say I love Him. I have gotten a lot of things wrong, but I was all in, seeking the One who was looking for me all along. Now that I am trying to get it right, it's not only me that's all in. I'm all in with Christ. He's all in with me, lifting my broken love to where it wants so eagerly to go. He has seen everything that I have ever done, and He has loved me, mended me, made me shine with His Life and allowed me to love with His love.

I wanted to weave you a tapestry to cover over my life with the sacred story of St. Photini. But the truth is that both of us share the strength of being uncovered, out there, drawing water in the midday brightness. Our tapestries are all given over to keeping other people warm. But we're both right here, seen straight through by Christ. When He showed us who we really are by revealing who He really is, we were both all in. Christ loves women like us. Not because we did wrong in the battle fog of trying to survive, but because we love out loud and will run to Christ when we get the scent of Water.

REFLECTION QUESTIONS

1) Are you avoiding living a full life because you feel you aren't living up to the 'norm?' Not part of the 'mom, dad, kids, dog, and white picket fence picture?' Jesus knew Photini was worthy. Do you really believe you are not just as worthy?

2) Are you willing to have an encounter with Christ to listen to what he has to say, and change what you don't like?

3) What 'well of earthly pleasures' do you keep going to that never quite satisfies? Do you keep doing the same thing and expecting something to change?

4) Are you ripe for the harvest? If not, come to the well and ask for the living water and it will be given to you just as freely as to Photini. Then be ready and willing to be used for his glory. Think about what your gifts might be. We know you have them, God said so in Romans 12:6-7, and we know he keeps his promises. A note on gifts: Sometimes we may not recognize our own gifts. The next time someone asks you to do something for or with them, prayerfully consider your answer. Don't just say no right away because you think it is not your gift. Remember as we read in Luke 10:1-2 that the 70 were called, they didn't volunteer! Like Photini, you too can be an unlikely but beautiful example to your family, friends and strangers.

Illustration

SAINT SOPHIA & HER THREE DAUGHTERS FAITH, HOPE, & LOVE
MARTYRED 126 A.D.

To Be a Pilgrim

SAINT HELEN
REPOSED 328 A.D.

Elissa Bjeletich Davis

BACK WHEN I THOUGHT I was happily -- or at least, durably -- married, I was writing a children's lesson about St. Constantine and his mother, St. Helena. As I read through a synopsis of her life, the word 'divorce' caught my attention. Sometime after Constantine was born, her husband (not yet an Emperor) left Helena for a more advantageous match, to better scale the social ladder. My mind lit up. *Perfect! St. Constantine had a single mom, and he loved her and honored her again and again. I'll emphasize this for kids whose parents are divorced. They'll see themselves in the Saints! Wonderful.*

Shortly thereafter, as my marriage unraveled, I watched St. Helena from the corner of my mind. I was struggling to save the marriage -- holding on with all my strength, really. I was praying to St. Anna, St. Nicholas, and anyone who seemed to have experience saving marriages. But not Helena. She was divorced.

I'm stubborn and strong-willed, though I prefer to see myself as resolute and strong. My mom stayed in a bad marriage to the very end, and though I could see her mistake, I couldn't see mine, and I hung in there like a champ. I had consecrated myself fully to this marriage, and I couldn't imagine letting go. Eventually, the choice was made for me. Even as I let go, I knew this was a *get out of jail free* card; I knew that I wouldn't have ended the marriage myself, but I was going to be a lot better off without it.

Enter Helena.

When I finally relaxed my death grip on that marriage, I collapsed, exhausted. I was emptied out, scraped and raw -- like someone had cleaned me out with a melon baller. Holding on like that had cost me something. In my exhaustion and weakness, I watched my five kids grapple with their dad's exit. They were hurt and upset and torn up too, and I couldn't fix it for them. I had totally invested myself in creating this beautiful Orthodox upbringing for them. I was a homemaker, and now that home was in ruins. My life's work seemed to be disappearing. What would happen now? What if their dad left the Church entirely? Would they leave the Church too?

All of the stability and structure I had created for the kids crumbled. They were with dad half the time, every other week. They attended church half-time now. But the more critical and immediate problem (or as I was thinking, *disaster*) was that I couldn't manage to keep our structure even when they were in my home: morning prayers, evening prayers, dinner blessings -- they were all disappearing. I had once ensured that my home moved to an Orthodox rhythm, with a prayer cycle and family dinners and church on Sundays. But the rhythm was off now: not just the household rhythm, but my own internal rhythm, my prayer life and my routines, had simply vanished. I had let go of the rope and it got away from me -- and I could not get it back. I worried about their spiritual lives. How would these kids, lacking those rhythms, develop the faith that I had so hoped to foster?

And then she came to my mind. St. Helena came to mind, and this time I looked squarely at her and realized that she had been in a situation like this, and she would be here with me as I walked through this. I was encouraged: *her son became a saint.* Constantius left her after twenty years together for another woman, and their son moved to his pagan home. Helena had to feel cast aside like I did, and she must have seen, like me, that after years of raising a child with a warm, Christian maternal influence, she no longer had any control over his rhythms and influences. Young Constantine, not yet an Emperor, was to shadow his powerful uncle, Diocletian. He would study under him, learning to be a great leader so that he might take his own position of power one day. What an influence for a young man! Constantine would learn at the side of the cruelest persecutor of Christians. How did Helena absorb all of this? This was a woman I needed to get to know.

I went back to my books, to the various "Saints' Lives" that described her. As her life unfolded before me, I started to recognize details. Her life was not so unlike mine -- a worse version of it, of course, intensified by the high rank of her ex-husband and the times in which she lived, but not so different.

Like me, Helena met her beloved when she was a young woman. She lived in the third and fourth centuries, so the details can be foggy, but we do know that Eutropius indicates that she was born out of wedlock[1]. Ambrose writes,

> They claim that at first she was hostess of an inn, and known as such to the elder Constantine, who afterwards secured the realm. Good hostess, who so diligently sought for the manger of the Lord. Good hostess who did not ignore that host, who cared for the wounds of the man wounded by robbers. Good hostess who preferred to be considered dung, to gain Christ. For that reason Christ raised her from dung to a kingdom, as it is written that "He raised up the needy from the earth, and lifted up the poor out of the dunghill."[2]

So, Helena worked in an inn, and perhaps one evening while she was getting drinks and sweeping floors, Constantius walked in. It's impossible now to piece together how the story went, but it seems to me that they must have been in love at some point. (How funny -- I could say the same thing about myself: we were in love once, right? It seems that we must have been, as I peer through that fog.) Constantius was of a higher social status than Helena, so instead of a legal marriage, they lived in "concubinage". Apparently, at the time it stood to reason that an important or well-born man might live as

---

[1] Eutropius, Brev. 10.2
[2] Ambrose, *De obitu Theodosii (395)*, 42.

husband and wife, sharing a home and having children, with a woman of low stature, but legal marriage was reserved for women of a better class.

So, the innkeeper's daughter lived together with the more regal Constantius, and in 274, they had a son. While they weren't married legally, they had a serious, socially acceptable commitment to one another -- maybe it was something like a common law marriage. Constantius stayed until either 289 or 294, depending on who you ask. They were together for perhaps 20 years when Constantius found a woman who was better suited, apparently, to become an Empress. Theodora came from a nobler family, and could better help him achieve his ambitions.

My kids came home from their dad's house having so enjoyed their time with his new girlfriend and her kids. They wore clothes handed down from her, laughed at group texts she sent. It stung. I know that it's better that the kids love this new woman, and that it would be terrible if she were mean and scary, but it stung. On holidays, he invited all the same people for the same meals we had once made together, but I had been plucked out of the picture and replaced by another woman. In my depression and sadness, I began to think that perhaps he was right, that she was just better than I was. I began to think he was right to replace me.

I thought of Helena. How did Constantius tell her that he was leaving? Had he been a faithful mate for all of those years, or had he always been involved with other women on the side? Had she anticipated such a thing happening, or did she imagine that the two of them would grow old together? Did she imagine that all of her love and support would satisfy him, and keep him home? Did it sting when he married Theodora? Did Helena begin to think that maybe Theodora was a better fit, maybe she was just better all around? Did it get as dark for Helena as it did for me?

I began to ask Helena all of these questions, and to ask that she somehow pass to me the strength that carried her through those days. And I began to think about what she would have done to steady herself. Surely, she prayed. Helena was a devout Christian, prayerful and good. Her story doesn't follow that pattern we see all too often in the lives of female saints: *she was a beautiful young woman, and the powerful pagan man demanded that she succumb to his desires, but she refused, declaring that her truest love was the Lord Jesus Christ, and nothing could make her marry a pagan! Then they killed her, and she lives in eternal glory with a martyr's crown.* It's hard for me to relate to these immaculate virgin martyrs that seem to make up the majority of female saints. Helena is different. She didn't refuse Constantius because he was a pagan, but embraced him and lived out twenty years of her life beside him. She was a Christian in the real world, in a way. She was surrounded by pagans, and she must have gotten along well with them, but in her heart, she was always holding tight to Christ.

And then, at the height of the Roman persecution of Christians, led by her own brother-in-law, the much-despised Emperor Diocletian, her son would go away to join the persecutors. He would witness Diocletian's terrible scenes. Was Constantine there when Diocletian had the beautiful Julitta beaten with rods while her little son looked on? When he took Cyricus on his lap but the boy broke free, shouting, "Let me go to my mother, I am a Christian." Diocletian threw the boy down from the tribunal and kicked him down the stone steps. Did Constantine also look on as Julitta watched him die, there on the ground? Constantine must have witnessed so much cruelty as he followed his uncle. What was he thinking as he compared the peaceful Christian faith of his mother to the terrors his pagan uncle was inflicting?

When Constantius died, leaving Constantine to rule his quarter of the Roman Empire, Constantine made a bold move, declaring an end to the persecution of Christians under his rule. The other three emperors, including Diocletian, were outraged and began to move against him. This was no small issue -- Constantine was disrupting the entire empire, creating a sort of civil war and putting his own life and position on the line, to end the persecution.

I think of Constantine, and how his love and respect for his mother must have influenced this, the decisive and defining action of his life. He battled the other emperors and won, again and again, fighting under the sign of the cross. Ultimately, Constantine gained the entire Western half of the empire, and Licinius, governing the Eastern half, joined him in signing the Edict of Milan, ending the great Roman persecution of Christians. Christians would come out of hiding, building churches and holding councils, and our Church as we know it would begin to take its shape.

All of this, because a divorced and abandoned mom offered a good enough example of Christian love to her son. In the later years, she couldn't be there, but the memory of her and the influence of her faith, made all the difference.

I asked Helena if perhaps I should stop agonizing over the rhythm of my home, and focus on being a beautiful example to my own children. Perhaps, if they could see God at work inside of me as Constantine saw it in his mother, they too would be drawn to Him. My role was not just to set the rhythms, but to set the example. I began to rest easier, to focus on praying for my kids and for myself, instead of fretting over the prayer schedules and routines. Those might come back in good time, but I could trust that God moves mountains and He moves hearts. Like Constantine, perhaps my children most needed to see their mother's faith and love.

As my heart relaxed a bit, I began to reawaken. No longer dominated by fear of the unknown, my mind had room to start taking stock. I began to ask myself why I had chosen this particular man, which took me down a path: who was I when I met him? What were my priorities, my dreams, my interests? As I tried to understand my marriage, I started to see again the person I was before I married. For two decades I had been a wife and a mother, and maybe I lost track of that girl who fell in love and wanted to start a family. What else did she want? And as she came into focus, I began, for the first time, to want to be that person again.

Going back to my youth means going back to St. Helena. Literally. I grew up in a very rural area of California, outside of town, but with a St. Helena address. For the early years of my life, St. Helena was where you'd find the high school, the grocery store, and a lovely Main Street full of historic buildings and ice cream shops. Growing up outside the Church, I was only vaguely aware that St. Helena must have been a person, and I didn't much ask myself how she became our patron saint.

As it turns out, our town was named after the nearby Mount Saint Helena, and that the mountain was actually named independently by three different people -- but they always chose the same name. In 1823, a Catholic priest named Fr. Altimira was busy, founding Mission Sonoma, and one day while he was resting, he gazed upon the beautiful mountain, whose shape looks like a reclining woman. As he considered the curves of the mountain, he was reminded of a carving of St. Helena he had seen in France, at the Abbey of Rheims. Struck by the resemblance, he announced the name: Mount Saint Helena, or rather, he probably named it something more Spanish, like Santa Elena.

It seems that the mountain was not 'officially' listed on maps by its new name by the time Baron Alexander Rotchef visited Fort

Ross in 1841, the Southernmost outpost of the Russian fur traders, located on the opposite side of the mountain from Fr. Altimira's Catholic mission. He brought along his adventurous wife, the Russian Princess Helena, goddaughter to Czar Nicholas himself. The Princess happily joined an expedition of Russians exploring the mountain, and when they reached the top, the party named the mountain for the Princess' patron saint, Helena. Perhaps the name would have been something like Svyatoy Yelena?

Finally, a third person 'discovered' the lovely ladylike mountain. This time, a seafaring man named Capt. Stephen Smith came on his ship, the St. Helena, to his coastal land grant near Bodega Bay, where he would establish a redwood sawmill and would declare the name of the beautiful mountain in the distance to be Mount Saint Helena, after his beloved boat.

So, it's local legend that the mountain was independently named three times, by people who did not know each other. It's too much for coincidence. This name, Mount Saint Helena, must be somehow ordained by God -- a promise, perhaps, that the Empress does watch over the people there. All the while, I managed to grow up under her gaze without realizing -- or caring -- about that colorful past, and this triple connection to a Byzantine Empress.

St. Helena was still a place to me, not a person, even as I named my third child Helena -- after her sharp, funny great aunt Helen. But as Helena grew and began to ask about her name-Saint, she began to take shape for me, in beautiful icons and soon, in my prayers. My Helena was born with a cleft lip and palate, and through her many surgeries, I would call on a whole list -- a dream team -- of Saints, among them Helena. As I asked her to watch over this child, I slowly inched toward her, ever so gently sliding into knowing her.

As I learned more about Orthodoxy, St. Helena's story began to take shape -- mostly in her relationship to her son, St. Constantine, and in particular, in her discovery of the One True Cross. In my mind, she became the Empress Helena, the lovely crowned figure in her icons, holding up the cross for all the world to see. No longer a geographical location, St. Helena was the woman the Emperor sent to Jerusalem, seeking all of the holiest places and objects. Perhaps Helena was the first pilgrim to the Holy Land.

I'm always so delighted to see how God arranges things for us. I don't think He's a puppeteer, orchestrating every detail of our lives, but I do think that sometimes God sends experiences in what appears to be an organized order. Somehow, He offers an experience, and then I find that the knowledge and skills I picked up there turn out to be quite necessary for handling the next thing He throws at me. Sometimes I can even see it, discerning just what He did, how He lined everything up in the right order. I never know what's around the bend, but it would seem that God equips me, always providing and gently instructing.

For many years, my friend Whitney and I said that we'd take a pilgrimage to the Holy Land together. Now mind you, we say a lot of things. We are also going to walk the Camino Santiago in Spain, and then create a village of tiny houses where we can be beekeepers. We may also move to one of those abandoned Italian towns that will pay you to live in a villa. We have a lot of plans that I don't necessarily expect to come to fruition. One day, she told me that she'd received a small inheritance and was ready to use it on our Holy Land pilgrimage. I hadn't considered going so soon -- I guess I thought of it as a trip I could take when the kids were older and life was quieter. I certainly couldn't imagine dropping everything and going right at that moment. My marriage was on the rocks, my life was so busy and so hard -- but I could see that Whitney really felt like her grandmother had left her this money for a pilgrimage, and this was the time. This was God's time. He sent Whitney to nudge me along, and soon enough she and I were aloft on a flight to Israel.

When the Emperor Constantine sent his mother, the Empress Helena, to Jerusalem, he tasked her with following Christ's footsteps, acquiring the places He'd been and building great churches on each. Today, throughout the Holy Land, every church, monastery or shrine has a conspicuous icon of Helena. Most significantly, the street leading from the Christian Quarter in to the Holy Sepulchre of our Lord, the holiest place on earth, is named St. Helena Road. She is deeply beloved in this land.

The Theotokos is beloved in the Holy Land too -- both mothers, both offering a sort of quiet, unshakable example of beautiful faith in God. The Mother of God and the mother of the Emperor. Every day, Mary walked to the places where she last saw her Son, praying in the garden and preaching to crowds at the site of His ascension. Three hundred years later another mother arrived, marking those holy places with churches. You can feel the two women all over Jerusalem -- and so could St. Ambrose, as we can see:

> "Helen, then, came and commenced to look about the sacred places. The Spirit inspired her to search for the wood of the Cross, She drew near to Golgotha and said "Behold the place of combat, where is the victory? I seek the standard of salvation and I do not find it." [...] "How do I believe that I have been redeemed, if my redemption itself is not seen?"

> "I see what you did, O Devil, in order that the sword by which you were destroyed might be walled up. [...] Let the ruins be removed that life may appear; let the sword be drawn forth with which the head of the true Goliath was cut off; let the earth be opened that salvation may shine

forth. Why did you labor to hide the wood, O Devil, unless that you may be vanquished a second time? You were vanquished by Mary, who gave the Conqueror birth. She without detriment to her virginity, brought forth Him to conquer you by His crucifixion, and to subjugate you by His death. Today also you shall be conquered when a woman discovers your snares. As that holy one bore the Lord, I shall search for His cross. She showed Him created; I, raised from the dead. She caused God to be seen among men; I shall raise from the ruins the divine standard as a remedy for our sins.

[...] And as before Christ had visited a woman in Mary, so the Spirit visited a woman in Helen. He taught her those things which as a woman she knew not, and led her to the way which no mortal was able to know. [...] Mary was visited to liberate Eve; Helen was visited that emperors might be redeemed. [3]

I'm so interested in these parallels that St. Ambrose sees, and as I begin to search them and consider them, it strikes me that both of these holy women are in some way, mothers without husbands, ready to intercede for us and to help us find comfort and peace. I want to rest in both of them.

I love this idea that Mary brought us Christ created, incarnate, and Helena shows us Christ resurrected by revealing the Cross. Christ takes flesh from Mary, and somehow the resurrection takes on a physical presence in the Life-Giving Cross. One of the best things about pilgrimage to the Holy Land is how sharply the Incarnation comes into focus. It's not just that God took on flesh, but it's that His

---

[3] Ibid. 43-47

works and all of these Bible stories we have learned were also physical and real: Jacob lived here, and John the Forerunner stood there. So many of these locations overlap. For instance, Abraham led his son, Isaac, up the hill to sacrifice him in the very same spot where Christ was crucified. That connection illuminates the ways in which Isaac's walk up that hill with the wood of his death on his back is a foreshadowing of Christ's walk up Golgotha. God reaches out to us through prophets and saints, through Scriptures and icons, and even through geography. He never stops trying to touch us and to reveal Himself to us.

Helena is the first pilgrim, and by marking these sites and building these churches, she gives all of us the gift of pilgrimage. That's a tremendous gift. I feel like God gave me my pilgrimage to prepare me for my divorce. He loaded me up with awe and joy and deeper faith, knowing that I would need it in the months to come. He assured me that He is right here with me, really here, even in the geography and physicality of my world.

We toured through so many churches and monasteries, and ate in interesting cafes and met fascinating people. When finally our trip was winding down, we had one last stop. There is a bakery that provides all of the prosphora for all of the Greek Orthodox churches in Jerusalem and its environs. It's a little, ancient apartment in the Christian Quarter, and we followed a twisty, complex path through the maze of buildings to find it. There is a nun who runs this bakery, and she has the most amazing smile and truly does make the best bread you've ever tasted. The place is beautiful and she is delightful -- but it didn't seem like a particularly holy end to our trip. As we got ready to leave, I commented on the beautiful, cozy space, with its plaster walls and lovely arches. She turned to me and casually offered that this was St. Helena's apartment. When the Empress came to Jerusalem, this is where she stayed. My mind swirled. This was her apartment? Of course, it was. It's beautiful and lovely, and there are so many holy places in Jerusalem that you can't even enter a bakery without finding one. God sent me -- whose home is St. Helena -- to St. Helena's home.

And then I saw it. My whole life begins in St. Helena, which means that she has watched over me, the patron saint of my hometown, since before I even thought of her as a person. All of our lives are always pilgrimages toward the heavenly Jerusalem that awaits us. I began with St. Helena, and with her, I am a pilgrim on the road to Jerusalem. We have both seen the deep pain of divorce, and felt the way that our control as mothers slipped through our fingers. Helena kept on, and after the time of mourning and pain that she must have endured, she emerged with a son who loved Christ and truly battled for Him, and who honored her as the Empress. She made that journey to Jerusalem in a spiritual way and then in a physical way, literally creating a path for all of us to follow.

With her help, we can get there too.

REFLECTION QUESTIONS

1) How can I prepare the way for my children to be pilgrims, too?

2) Where is the Cross in my life? How can it restore me and my children to life?

3) Helen did not let great sorrow and rejection keep her from seeking God. What can you share with her so she can help you find God's face in your struggles?

Gathering Aunties

SAINT ANTHOUSA
REPOSED 407 A.D.

Elizabeth Gatling

IT'S FRIDAY NIGHT, and the doorbell rings. I'm wearing socks and a warm shawl over my comfy loungewear. I open the door to a front stoop filled with friends: a married couple, a single friend, a couple of married women who came alone, and a teenaged boy who came to play video games with my son. My son YonBoy, who did not grow under my heart but who has grown in my heart since 2007, comes downstairs and greets his friends and mine. YonBoy offers drinks around and helps me serve a few of the aunties before he and his friend head back to his room. He's grown up with aunties and into a consummate host. The teens retreat into their streaming, and I tell my friends about tonight's K-drama. We have time for three episodes before it gets too late and cold out for our arthritises and fibromyalgias, the aches of middle age.

Tonight's show, like several of the crowd favorites, features a chef as one of the main characters. My friends say, "Oh, man. This show makes me so hungry! Good thing we're at Beth's house, since she's such a great cook!" I don't disagree. I love to cook for people. The table in the next room is laden with snacks and a dinner I put together for everyone. They don't know it yet, but I made one of the dishes from tonight's show. They'll be hungry halfway through, and someone will notice then. For now, we gather in expectant silence as the opening credits roll. I look around at my friends and tilt my head to hear my son's deep voice from his room. He laughs, that surprise that never ceases to warm my heart ever since he was a little boy eating on my lap, and I glance toward the icon corner in silent thanks. The show starts, and we're drawn into the story of a woman with a past, just as that past catches up to her. Life isn't easy for the heroine and her child, but it looks like she might make it.

In a K-drama, there are tropes that have to be included in every plot arc: the moment when you eat with someone for the first time, cooking an elaborate holiday meal with friends, cooking a hodgepodge feast with foods from a gas station, taking care of someone when the weather gets bad, having someone observe something good about you in secret, cleaning house together, mixing generations in a side quest, wild trips to enjoy another part of the country, and long talks to the ancestors to express forgiveness and the need for help while you try to do your best.

My parenting journey has been a lot like a K-drama. Sometimes I cook gourmet meals with surprise tie-ins, and some seasons have felt like one long day after another of trying to make gas station food seem holy. And maybe I don't talk with my hereditary ancestors all that much, but I definitely ask my ancestors in the faith for help. All. The. Time.

What has helped me most has been that I haven't had to go it alone. Just like the characters in the shows I love, I have had friends at my tables, whether they were festal or paltry or just a cup and a cookie balanced on a knee in a park or a driveway. When I look at the mother of one of the most revered saints, I see a familiar pattern, too: St. Anthousa, the widowed single mother of St. John Chrysostom and his sister Pulcheria, gathered aunties into her home to help her rear her children. Not only that, but her life isn't that far off from some of the tragic parts of a K-drama heroine's backstory.

Saint Anthousa was married to a soldier, and as soldiers often do, he was killed in battle, leaving her with two small children, Pulcheria and John. Just like today, it was very hard to raise a child–especially a son–as a single woman. A single woman of a certain class. Her husband was an officer in the Roman army, which meant that she was probably of the lower nobility. There was money. There was a household. There were servants. She ran all of that expecting him to come home. And he didn't.

I can imagine that she was really stressed by this. In the K-drama version of her life, I bet there would be a montage as she tried to figure out how she was going to again run her household without the money coming in. I mean, they were probably fairly well off from what I've read, but you know: If money is constantly going out, and it's not coming back in, after a while it continues to dwindle. Even if there's a pension coming from the empire for his service. (In the K-drama, that pension would be set aside sacrificially for the boy's education, and the mother would pass up new clothes and social opportunities and even the option of getting remarried.) Raising a son in the Eastern Roman Empire would have been very difficult for a woman, because boys were raised so differently from girls at that time. Even with setting aside money for his future education, how was Saint Anthousa to teach John the basics that would get him there?

Education can be one of the hardest needs to supply when you're a single parent. My ex-husband insisted on homeschooling our son, even after we divorced. That demand to homeschool was very hard for me, because I was working full time. I had to bring money in to support the household I shared most of the time with my son. How was I going to homeschool my son, too? On the one hand, I'm intelligent. I'm not a teacher, but I know how to convey information. On the other hand (and two feet), I also have to work every day and take care of running the household.

What I realized was that I couldn't do it alone. (Don't let anybody tell you that you should do it alone.)

Saint Anthousa didn't do it alone. She had help. Her sister, or perhaps her sister-in-law–I'm not sure which– was a deaconess and a dedicated virgin. Her name was Sabiniana. She came to live with Anthousa and the children in order to help rear and teach them. Auntie Sabiniana also played a role later on in John's life after his mother died, traveling with him into exile and back.

I'm not saying that there's something wrong about how other church fathers talk about women, but there's definitely something right about how Saint John Chrysostom talks about women. He notices the dignities that they can rise to or fall from, and he sees the holiness in a woman managing a household in peace. I connect it with his life with a mother and aunties who loved him. (The K-drama version would have a split screen showing just that: Saint John Chrysostom up there wooing the crowds with his glowing sermons, while we see on the other side Anthousa and Sabiniana bowing to each other and choosing to give way to each other's strengths rather than bickering as the children tear around them acting like kids who've had too much sugar.) Mothers in his sermons aren't angels who give out peace without effort, with a word of command. They're real people who struggle but can find ways to live in peace and kindness together with the ones who help them. Y'all, that's a word that you need to hear.

Why do people think women can angelically raise kids without assistance? Like, really, who actually thinks that? If Anthousa was running a household (with all that entails), educating her children, having to feed people, *and* doing all the work that goes with being a head of household, how was she doing that alone? Answer? SHE WASN'T, and trying to convince people she did only sets an impossible standard for other mothers to reach for, especially since she has "Saint" right there in front of her name. It just sets up women for failure and a lot of pointed fingers if they try to reach a ridiculously impossible standard. She reared those children *with help.* Learning to live with aunties gave her more than enough room to grow personally, along with more than enough help. That little boy who saw his mama and aunties biting off their irritations in order to treat each other with respect no matter what is the man who gave us the Liturgy of Peace. He's the one who befriended deaconesses (in addition to his Auntie Sabiniana) and taught ordinary married women how to make their households carry the peace of the church, the peace of Christ, into the world.

In the montage of the K-drama of my life, you'll see me crying like every other heroine when my marriage ends and when I have to figure out again who I am, when I lose an ancestor and have to grieve alone and with a child. But you'll also see the sun shine out on me. One scene in the montage, I'll be chopping onions instead of crying from sadness, and the doorbell will ring. It will be taco night, and a group of friends will join my son and me at the table before the friends take my son outside to play while I have a nap or pay the bills. Another night I'll be out of gas, and other friends will pull up with a full gas can and a hug. My voiceover will tell you then that if you reach out, there will be all these aunties around that will help you raise your kids.

Women usually know how to reach out in theory, but we forget to ask sometimes because we live in a society right now that says, "Do it all yourself. Be independent. Pull yourself up by your bootstraps!" (which is an impossible task). No, the better thing is to be interdependent, and reach out to the women around you who have done it before. (The montage will switch to us cooking a big meal together, the aunties and I. Anthousa and Sabiniana are cooking in a parallel scene, and for a minute the screen overlaps them, so that it's like they're helping me, too.) Even women who are married can help you, because they're doing the same thing that you are doing. They have done it. They ARE doing it. They have experience. Let them help you. Let them be there for your children and for you. (The montage ends after we bow to each other at the door, and everyone goes home respected and full and satisfied by the food and the company.)

Between Anthousa and Sabiniana, John was given a classical education to the point that he was accepted as a student by the pagan Libanios, a famous teacher of rhetoric at Antioch. When he learned of Anthousa's courage and ability in raising her family alone, he looked around at his pupils and said: "Great heavens, what remarkable women are to be found among the Christians!" Imagine that. This teacher was so impressed by this teenage boy who came to him as a student that he praised *his mother*! And he praised her to other pagans! Frankly that means she did a bang-up job. And that puts me in mind of the words of Boaz to Ruth (Ruth 3:11) "... all the assembly of my people know that you are a worthy woman."

I've lived off of those words for years. When my plot twist came, it wasn't easy to believe that the assembly of God's people would know that I am a worthy woman. It wasn't easy for *me* to believe that I was a worthy woman! Rearing a child is hard! Who could be worthy of it? But just like in a K-drama, there are people who see the good you do, who see the good *of* you, even when you don't see it yourself.

Knowing that should give you hope that even in the midst of the hardest time of your life, the most difficult thing that you may ever do–which is have total and complete or almost total and complete responsibility for another human by yourself–that with the examples that are set before us and that great cloud of witnesses, you can be a worthy woman. You can become a worthy woman because you already are one. God has *called* you worthy. He called all of us worthy because he loves us.

That doesn't mean everything is going to be a walk in the park. At least, not without some plot twists thrown in! Kids will be kids. Teenagers will be teenagers–(oh, my gosh, don't get it twisted)– Teenagers will be Teenagers. They will push every button you have, because they know your buttons, because they've lived with you. Just like you know their buttons. But when you reach out for the help that is there–for God's hand, which will show up in the words and the actions of other worthy women and men–you will find that your child will be able to be safe enough at home to question things and unfurl the edges of themselves, testing not only your patience but also (and mostly) their wings. When they go out from your worthy home, they will go out with a foundation and understanding of what they should and should not do. You will not have to worry that they will not know or be able to express themselves.

I found now that I've met Anthousa that I am letting go of my desire to make my son in my image. I want him to grow into the man God has planned for him to be. I want him to have a safe space to come back to if he needs to. But these days I don't worry so much if he says he wants to leave and go somewhere and do something. Like Anthousa who gathered aunties and practiced the faith in her home, I've been striving all these years to live a worthy life with worthy aunties (and uncles) and saints (in the K-drama, you can see them, but I mostly just talk to them and follow their recipes as best I can). That's the big reveal here, in my life with God and Saint Anthousa. If we live the life that God expects in front of them, a life that isn't filled with our own efforts alone, that example will push teens towards being upright decent humans who love God and their fellow man.

It's the end of the episode, and my friends gasp at the plot twist that just unfolded. We head to the kitchen to refill drinks and plates before we start the next one. Someone notices the special dish. "So, wait. If Seo-Jun made this, then..." "YES!" we cackle together in what will become another of a thousand inside jokes borne of this life together. My son comes into the room, drawn by the laughter. His eyes smile the way mine smile, keeping a laugh inside to warm him before letting it out. It's not the only thing he gets from me, but I love to see it.

There are times when my son is the epitome of patience and grace far beyond his age and whacked out circumstances. And then there are moments like tonight, when he's lit from within by a smile that tells me just what I need to know. This life, this worthy life, has given him ballast. Maybe his world is not as stable as some, but he has what he needs to balance. He has this food, this mother's prayers, these saints, these friends, these aunties.

REFLECTION QUESTIONS

1) Are you trying to rear your children on your own? Think of three people you can ask for help or companionship in three things.

2) What shows or music or hobbies or cuisines do you enjoy? Have you considered sharing them with friends and acquaintances as a way to build community?

3) Are there any tropes that help you understand your life? Can you see your hopes and desires and struggles in any lives of saints?

4) What do you think helped Anthousa and Sabiana get along so well that they set an example of peace in their home?

A Map of Tears & Flowers

SAINT MONICA
REPOSED 387 A.D.

Kristina Roth

"READ THE PARAKLESIS to the Theotokos every day. Pray to St. Monica. Pray to St. Helen."

Short and slightly stooped, the abbess gave me this advice in her heavy Greek accent. We sat in the autumn sunshine behind the catholicon at her monastery. Giant wooden crates of green apples sat further back in the shade, plump and luminous, picked from their orchard and waiting to be served to pilgrims.

I'd mustered courage to speak with her, this busy, sometimes gruff leader of a thriving convent. I didn't want to inconvenience her. But anxiety about a likely divorce and becoming a single mom made me bold, even as others waited, noticeably impatient, for their chance to seek her advice.

I was already leaning on many: Christ, the Theotokos, Saints Esther, Xenia, John Maximovitch, Paisios, Elizabeth the New Martyr, Gabriel, Joachim and Anna, Nicholas, Seraphim, George, Joseph, Cristina. And every one of them helped.

But I had never heard of St. Monica. After the abbess' advice, I did some cursory research. Raised a Christian in North Africa, she was nevertheless married to a pagan man who openly chased other women and scorned her faith. After his death, she raised three children on her own. My intercessions to her were brief and haphazard that first year.

Now, several years later, finally taking the time to seek her out, what I read about her pulls me back to the tumultuous transition of raising a boy on my own and the ongoing journey of doing so.

St. Monica is typically overshadowed by her son St. Augustine, whose writings are well known. Nonetheless, he gives her and her prayers for him much credit for his eventual faith and knowledge of the truth. Her spiritual fervor was great, marked by daily attendance at services, generous offerings, and unceasing prayer –

especially for her son, who pursued heresies and lived with a woman he wasn't married to. All the while, she prayed.

When my son's father decided he wanted to end our marriage of fifteen years, I knew I wouldn't make it through without immense spiritual support. Fear and uncertainty drove me deeper into my faith than I even knew was possible. Friends took me to monasteries. My priest patiently met with me weekly while I cried and tried to understand my role in the situation. Countless people, and saints, prayed for me.

And I prayed, too, more than ever. My copy of the paraklesis service to the Theotokos became worn as I read it in waiting rooms or at home sitting on the floor before my icons. The struggles and triumphs of the saints become relevant to me in personal ways. For many years I had prayed, "Lord, draw me closer to you." When we became Orthodox, I continued to pray, "I believe; help thou my unbelief." I believed, but for decades, my faith felt weak, tender little sprouts of belief whose roots were still shallow. It took the devastation of having my world turned upside down to establish it more fully, sink the roots further.

St. Monica also knew that the intense prayers spurred by emotional devastation could help grow wobbly seedlings into strong ones. With the wisdom of hindsight, her son wrote about her anguish over his spiritual choices before her prayers eventually helped draw him to God: "How comes it, then, that such sweet fruit is plucked from life's bitterness, the sweetness of groans, tears, sighs and laments?" (60) You, Lord, heard her petition and did not overlook her tears with which she watered the earth wherever she prayed."

That first year of upheaval into single parenthood, as painful as it was, was also a time of blessings. Never before had I sought God so earnestly or seen him work so obviously in my life.

But with the divorce, I had to leave the spiritually rich environment of where we then lived to return to my beloved, if remote, hometown where I could raise my son near family. This decision, practical as it was, uprooted me from the fertile spiritual environment of monasteries and weekly confession and regular services and spiritual support. I came home because South Dakota is a good place for a child to grow up. And I knew his father wouldn't be staying in California, either. Life has proven simpler and more manageable here, as I knew it would. But sometimes I wonder if I made the right choice. Should I have moved us instead to be near a larger parish or a monastery?

Because, as sweet as it is, our parish here is tiny. A priest comes about once a month from two states down. We have lay services on the other Sundays, sometimes with the immense blessing of reserved sacrament when our bi-vocational deacon can be with us. Often, my son is the only child there. The others who do come are much younger than him. This reality doesn't sit well with him, nor me. There is no church school program, limited fellowship opportunities. If I had more time, I would oversee such efforts. But motherhood and work require what energy I have.

Ultimately, of course, I know that the most effective way to nurture spiritual growth and learning is for it to happen in the home. I struggle to know how to best pass the faith to my son, how to set an example of spiritual life and demonstrate a steady relationship with Christ that will nourish his own growth. The truth is that the onus really is on me to teach him the faith, as it is with all parents. Of course, there are resources, thanks to the internet and modern publishing. But it's not always as easy as that. I feel frustrated. I want more help to teach him spiritual truths than I get. I haven't been able to visit a monastery in five years and he can't remember the last time he was at one. I pray that I can labor on as faithfully as St. Monica did with her prayers, not just for my son, but for myself as well.

***

Six years into my journey as a solo parent, I finally read the confessions of St. Monica's famous son so I could learn more about her. I was struck by the questions St. Augustine asked himself and asked God. His mother, like mothers everywhere, often felt exasperated with him and his endless questions, his pursuit of heresies as he tried to find truth. I don't think she was exasperated with his questions as much as she was with his refusal to see the truth. Of course, we can't force anyone to see the truth. All we can do is pray. And I think she knew this, too.

My son asks questions that I can't answer. Like many children, his questioning began around age three, and it hasn't stopped. "What is love? How do I really know I love someone?" he asked at age eight. My explanations didn't help much, although he was clearly impressed with 1 Corinthians 13. "Why are there so many different protestant churches? Why don't most of them have sacraments, and how are Roman Catholic sacraments different than Orthodox ones? Why aren't there more Orthodox people in our town?" There are other questions, too, even harder ones.

At age nine, he converses comfortably with his pediatrician (duly impressed) about how and why the picture of the black hole isn't really a picture of it. He talks fluently about planets and exoplanets, having surpassed my knowledge of astronomy in kindergarten. In fourth grade, he writes short stories that are better than any fiction I've attempted, charting out how many words he wants each chapter to be and planning the plot. I pray all of this curiosity will continue to have room for spiritual questions and perhaps, eventually, his own apologetics for the faith, just as St. Augustine's relentless questioning eventually did. He already sees and understands truths that I likely never will and this knowledge will only deepen as he grows.

When my boy was born, I thought I'd be able to rely on his dad to answer some of the big questions as he grew up, to defend the faith against atheism and relativism, to make the argument for trying to live a moral life even when it's hard and everything around you is fighting against it. After all, he had helped me answer my own unrelenting existential questions when we were young adults. Wouldn't he do the same for our son?

Did St. Monica ever feel like this as her son grew, doubtless full of his own questions? Did she wish she had more answers, or that his father helped more? I am learning that prayer is often the best answer, as she and her son also learned.

**

When he was two, my boy and I went into our open garage to blow bubbles, wanting to be out of the house but not fully in the sun of the suburban Houston heat. I turned my back and he darted into the house. My heart sank as I heard the deadbolt turn in the lock. I didn't realize he had the dexterity to work the knob.

I didn't have a key hidden under a flower pot or the door mat. My phone, of course, was behind the locked door. And his father worked thirty minutes away in the city, longer if traffic was bad.

I knocked on the door and called his name, encouraging him to open the door. But he didn't. Not wanting to be out of earshot, but also not willing to wait for hours until his dad came home, I dashed to a neighboring house. No one answered there, but someone did at the second. Phone call made, I returned to sit next to the locked door, talking to my son and hoping he could hear me, until his father arrived with a key. We found him in the living room contently playing with his Duplos.

Years later, I read an essay by another mom who had the same experience. She didn't wait for help, but instead decided to smash a window to get back into her house and ensure her child's safety. Breaking a window did cross my mind during that hot summer day while I waited in the garage. But I envisioned shards and crumbs of glass forever hiding in the carpet, waiting to bury themselves in our hands or feet.

Solo motherhood has created a ferocity, though, that wouldn't make me hesitate to break a window if I had to. Raising him on my own has led to a single-minded focus that perhaps I didn't have when married. Someone has to try to do it right, and that someone has to be me. There are always windows to be broken, even if metaphorically, and I hope my prayers will do that, just as St. Monica's did.

Last summer, years after that locked-door incident, the same sense of panic about my child being trapped returned. He spends every summer, all summer, with his father out of state. While in previous summers it had just been them, he now spends three months living in a family situation that doesn't set the example I'd hoped he would have. Even though he's not a toddler locked in a house alone, I feel even more helpless than I did then. But I can't call his father for help now.

Sending him away each summer feels harder every year.

St. Monica's situation was even harder than mine, though. How did she, in her obviously very deep attachment to her son, handle his far-flung travels? How did she manage those times when he left again without telling her beforehand? She had no phones, no video chats, no app to track his location, not even a reliable postal service. My heart seizes and my stomach knots up to imagine being so utterly out of touch with my beloved boy.

Even when St. Augustine did come home, there were always more trips to take. On one of his departures, as usual, his mother did not want him to leave. She followed him with tears and pleas to the shore. So, he tricked her, encouraging her to stay overnight at a holy place and telling her he would meet her in the morning so they could sail together. But instead, he left earlier than she knew, on a different ship to a different location, leaving her heartbroken and bereft when she went to port to sail.

I am absolutely certain St. Augustine knew how this would pain her. Unlike her, though, I try not to let my boy know how hard it is for me when he leaves every summer. He needs time with his dad and I want to support that, despite different lifestyles. So summer becomes a deeper season of prayer, more than any other time of year, as I count down the weeks until he returns.

Later, St. Augustine saw God's hand at work even in this deceitful escape of his. He wrote, "In your deep wisdom you acted in her truest interests: you listened to the real nub of her longing and took no heed of what she was asking at this particular moment, for you meant to make me into what she was asking for all the time. . . . Like all mothers, though far more than most, she loved to have me with her, and she did not know how much joy you were to create for her through my absence."

He was talking about his mother's aching desire that he come to the true faith, and how his journey was one step along the way to that conversion. She didn't realize that these constant separations from him, despite their pain, were necessary steps as God worked in St. Augustine's heart and led him to faith.

What joys will come through my son's necessary summer absences? It is hard to imagine. It may take years to know. I hope they bring fruit for both of us.

***

Life is more stable now with several years of solo motherhood under my belt. It's easy to forget to cling to the saints like I once did. I don't have as much free time to pray because I am working full time and raising a child singlehandedly. It's easy to assume that the breathtaking blessings that happened during my year of intense spiritual struggle will not be repeated (even though they have been).

A wall of icons overlooks our kitchen table and more are in the bedrooms. But actually praying before them is hard. It's not for lack of wanting. Rather, it's from the all-consuming exhaustion of doing everything, all the things, on my own. It can feel impossible to connect one thought to the next by the time I'm home after work and late school pickup, much less direct our spiritual lives, lead daily prayers, read the lives of the saints.

Working, parenting, home tending, yard caring, putting my wedding ring back on as a ruse when repairmen come to the house because I've been hit on by them too many times, taking appliances apart on my own, white knuckled driving to school on steep icy roads after dark because he has to stay for aftercare while I work, shopping, errand running, extracurricular activities, answering complicated questions about elementary school friendships and theology and science: these are the things that single moms navigate on our own.

I often feel like I have failed miserably when it comes to our spiritual lives, as though our icons are just decorations. Somehow, though, we always pray once he's tucked into bed. I sing the trisagion hymn and other songs in the dark. Sometimes his voice joins mine. His prayers are heartfelt and sweet. We often do this over the phone when he's away for the summer. I won't sing alone in public, but I put this discomfort aside to sing over the phone, not caring who might hear my voice on speaker, as long as he hears the songs.

It's tempting to think it was much easier for St. Monica to maintain her prayer life. She had maidservants, after all. She didn't have to deal with the hassles of housework and employment. Churches and shrines were everywhere around her. Priests were readily available for confession and spiritual council. I admit to envy – not just for her spiritual supports, but also for the mentorship that her son had from St. Ambrose.

As I learn about St. Monica, I realize I need her intercessions not just for my role as a mother, but for my own weak faith. Her relevance seems even greater now that I am several years into my journey as a single mother, especially as an Orthodox Christian without the fertile spiritual environment I once had. I find myself wishing I would have taken the time to learn more about her sooner, back when the abbess told me to pray to her.

But it's not too late to start coming to her more earnestly, asking that she will intercede for my son, for myself, for all of us as we wade through the heresies and false gods and confusion that surround us. Likewise, I'll ask her to intercede that my spiritual strength will return, that somehow my faith will be refreshed and reinvigorated despite not having monasteries nearby to visit or even weekly services with a priest.

Sometimes children that I know ask why their prayers aren't answered. It's hard to know how to respond. I explain that I have seen it take years, decades even, for some of my prayers to be answered. Life is like a connect-the-dot puzzle, I say. Some things have to occur before other things can come. But explaining that to a vulnerable, wide-eyed youngster isn't easy. Seeing how prayers are eventually answered is a lived, personal experience that involves patience and time, as much as I wish it weren't always that way.

***

When he was young, I began working on a series of botanical and seed photographs. It was an art form I could easily do while we played in the backyard. Pink magnolias, azaleas, camellias, peach and citrus and almond blossoms filled my California neighborhood.

I've continued to work on this series in South Dakota, turning instead to northern-climate plants, which aren't always as exuberant as their southern cousins. I have learned to look more closely for potential subjects: native prairie plants, perennials, seed bearing trees at the park. Last spring I dissected ovaries of tulips and daffodils from my garden for my photos. Daffodil ovaries are particularly luscious - plump, round, and green, full of tiny white eggs that stuck to my fingers as I arranged them for my photos. These eggs were as small as the dots on those connect-the-dot puzzles. Motherhood is like this, tiny seeds that grow in our bodies, our hearts, and then spring forth to mature on their own in ways we won't always be able to see for years.

We often hear that motherhood is martyrdom. We bear fruit and nurture it not just with our own bodies but also with years of physical work, emotional work, and, hopefully, spiritual work. We blossom in order to produce fruit, and then the fruit produces its own seeds in turn. Like St. Monica, I ache to see seeds of spiritual truth take root not only in my son, but of all the children I know and love.

***

Prayer is a long game. It's like starting an entire orchard from seeds instead of from saplings. It can take decades to see it come to fruition.

St. Monica reminds me to fervently focus on what matters, to never stop praying. To have faith. To keep planting seeds, no matter how tiny, no matter if those seeds are only single-word prayers that I remember to mutter while I'm falling asleep. She's not only for moms parenting solo. She's for all of us in this crazy post-Christian world, when even adults who were once strong in their beliefs leave the faith they grew up with, if they were fortunate to even hear about God at all. The culture around her was no less full of spiritual confusion.

Sometimes I wonder, though, if St. Monica was always so devout, or if there was something about motherhood that deepened the spark of faith within her. I can say that motherhood, in its own way, saved me. Single or not, the responsibility of raising a child has pushed me to become a stronger, more capable version of myself. And, most importantly, wanting my son to know Christ has led to deeper faith in myself. I find myself thinking that perhaps Augustine saved her in the same way. Would her faith have been as strong, as persistent, if she didn't have a wayward son, an unbelieving husband? If she didn't have a son at all?

In the end, of course, St. Monica's hopes for her son prevailed, through her prayers, through Christ's power. Her faith came full circle; her son's faith ripened to maturity. And it wasn't just her son's faith that matured, it was also her grandson's. Augustine writes like a proud father of Adeodatus's brilliance, wisdom, faith, and attractiveness. But he knows he can take credit for none of it; he gives all the credit to God: "Nothing did I contribute to that boy's making except my fault. It was you, and you alone, who had inspired us to instruct him in your truth as he grew up." (180)

I'd venture that St. Monica's entreaties, though, had something to do with this spiritual heritage. Her grandson died while yet a teenager, but Augustine does not write a prayer for future generations to say for his son as he did for his mother. Rather, he says, "I remember him without anxiety, for I have no fear about anything in his boyhood or adolescence." (180)

While Adeodatus's story is hardly mentioned in his father's autobiography, the few paragraphs about him are proof of St. Monica's legacy. As my son nears middle school, it's finally occurred to me to start praying about a possible future wife for him, any grandchildren I might have. I want the same legacy that she had. And the fact that her son's works have remained published and read for 1600 years after their earthly existence, pointing others to Christ, are also proof of her legacy.

She did this, Christ moving through her prayers, even when the culture was against her, even when her children's father took no spiritual responsibility, embraced adultery, treated her harshly. It was her, and Christ in her.

After St. Monica's repose, St. Augustine wrote a beautiful prayer for her, hoping that others throughout history would continue to bring her memory before God's altar. Her prayers came full circle as her son grew to love her as much as she had loved him, to be as concerned about his mother's salvation as she had been for his. It is a thing of beauty:

Forgive her, Lord, forgive, I beg you, and do not arraign her before you. Let mercy triumph over judgment, for you, whose utterances are true, have to the merciful promised mercy. Since their very power to be merciful was your gift to them in the first place, you will be showing mercy to those with whom you have yourself dealt mercifully. . . Let no one wrench her away from your protection. Let no lion or dragon thrust in between by force or guile; for she will not claim that she has no debts to pay, lest she be convicted by the crafty accuser and fall into his power; she will reply only that her debts have been forgiven by him to whom no one can repay what he paid for us, though he owed us nothing. (196)

***

On a recent trip to deliver my boy to his dad for the summer, I saw my first banyan tree, gigantic, limbs twisted around limbs, draping down and rooting into the soil to create a maze of itself. With curiosity, we gathered some of its small, red berries fallen to the moist ground. The seeds inside were so tiny you'd never guess they'd give life to one of the biggest trees on earth. Christ, the angels, and the saints, Monica included, prop me up like that, encircling me with their arms that reach down to the ground and become anchors. They do this for all of us. The tiny seeds of my feeble prayers and those of whoever pray for me sprout and grow wildly.

Each May, before he leaves for the summer, we plant flowers, some of them seeds, some of them seedlings. "They will be big when you get back," I tell him. Throughout the summer's heat, I water them. I prune and pluck spent blossoms and add steer manure, save my bunny's droppings for my young peonies. If I know hail is coming, I cover them. When he comes back, they are heavy with flowers. Last summer, I measured the length of his absence by how tall my giant sunflowers grew each week. By early October, the flowers have gone to seed. I gather these seeds – columbine, cosmos, hollyhock, coneflower, morning glory, and more – and tuck them away for next year.

References in this chapter from:

Augustine, Saint, and Maria Boulding. *The Confessions*. New York: Vintage Books, 1998.

REFLECTION QUESTIONS

1) What are the prayers you have been praying the longest for your child[ren]? Praying is like growing an orchard from seed. Have you seen growth from your prayers, even if it's slow?

2) Separation from children can be as painful as bearing the full brunt of their questions can be overwhelming. What in Saint Monica's story gives you hope in either of these experiences?

3) Do you have big questions? Does your child? What are some ways you can share the joy of seeking answers?

Shelter for the Shunned

SAINT MARGARET OF CORTONA
REPOSED 1297 A.D.

Carrie Chuff

MY PARENTS DIVORCED when I was eight. My memories from that time in my life are somewhat fuzzy, but the details I do remember are imbedded as if in stone. I attended a Catholic school at the time, and I remember one of the teachers, upon hearing what happened, being extraordinarily kind to me. She offered me stickers from her office if I ever felt down and needed a boost. "It's okay to cry," she said. "Don't let anyone tell you that you aren't strong if you cry."

I didn't cry very much about it, though, and I never did go back to her office for more stickers. My own feelings about my parents' divorce were—and still are—complex, but one of the things I remember most about that time was what happened around me, most particularly how it concerned my mother. She had custody of us, and so my siblings and I continued living with her at our home, though things were very different now. We had been active at our Catholic parish, the one connected to the school I attended. After the divorce, my friendships from church seemed to dry up. I saw these friends at school, of course, but for some reason they didn't come over to our house anymore. It didn't take me long to put two and two together, even at that young age. They didn't come to our house anymore because my parents were divorced. We became like outcasts, and if it was felt by me, I can only imagine how much more keenly it was felt by my mother.

Eventually that shunning led to becoming less active at church. The place where many go to find comfort and solace in their time of need became the source of even more pain for my mother. We didn't really go to church on Sundays anymore, and although my faith stayed intact, it went through many rocky periods. A particularly wonderful teacher in seventh grade helped bring about a spiritual renewal in my heart. From that year on, I gave myself completely to God and clung to my faith with everything I had. This inspired me to discern a vocation to become a nun, and I held on to that conviction all throughout high school, as well.

Initially, I was resolved to become a Carmelite nun, in the tradition of great Catholic Saints like Teresa of Avila and Therese of Lisieux. After a few years, however, it became apparent that I'd do better at a convent with a more active apostolate (the work taken on by a community). Cloistered nuns like Carmelites have prayer and asceticism as their main work for the good of the Church, whereas some other communities take part in things like teaching, nursing, or other such professions, in addition to their daily prayer and community life.

My parents were skeptical, especially my mom. How could a teenager make the decision to lead such an unusual and austere life, with so many rules that would prevent regular contact with friends and family members? Knowing the long history of monastic life in the Church didn't help much. My mother, especially, tried to be as supportive as possible. Deep down, though, she hoped that I'd change my mind at some point.

My teachers, once they caught wind of the decision I was going to make, were not supportive at all. I remember one of them cornering me in the hallway and telling me how disappointed she was. "Why aren't you going to go to college first? It's irresponsible to enter a convent fresh out of high school!" she said. "You're a good student, and this will be a terrible waste!" Normally, this type of resistance would have stopped me in my tracks, but I was so strongly convicted that I needed to pursue religious life after high school that it only served to spur me on.

My senior year of high school, I found a beautiful little community of Sisters in the deep South, whose strong life of prayer in community, combined with an apostolate of hosting retreats and teaching the faith to those who visited, seemed like the perfect fit for me. Before long, I found myself two months after high school graduation, with my bags packed to enter the convent for what I thought would be the rest of my life.

Entering the convent was certainly a culture shock! I learned the ins and outs of community life, which was a bit disorienting at first. In time, however, I settled in and tried my best to live this new life. As Sisters who followed the Rule of St. Francis, we listened to excerpts from his Rule each day at meals, and we celebrated all the Franciscan Saints on the yearly liturgical calendar.

It was in this way that I became more acquainted with Saint Margaret of Cortona. Ever since my "reversion" to a fuller practice of my faith in seventh grade, I felt a strong pull toward penitential Saints. The rocky moments when my faith was at its lowest point came to my mind frequently, and I was so saddened by the path my life could have taken if I hadn't returned to a fuller practice of my faith. It felt to me as if God had lifted me up with His own hands, and I was forever humbled and grateful for it. I had felt God's mercy so strongly in my own life, that I gravitated toward Saints who experienced it strongly in their lives, as well. When I learned about Saint Margaret, I felt a closeness to her. Her story resonated with me, even if her life was very different from mine.

Born in 1247 to farmers in a small Tuscan village in Italy, Saint Margaret of Cortona's mother died when she was only seven years old. Two years later, her father remarried a woman who treated her cruelly. As Margaret grew older, she became more reckless, and at the age of seventeen, she became the mistress of a young nobleman who lived near Montepulciano. For nine years, she lived in his castle, and their affair became common knowledge to the townspeople. During that time, she also bore him a son.

Margaret was granted many favors by her lover, including expensive clothing and a horse of her own, and her presence caused a great deal of scandal around Montepulciano. She was faithful to the man she loved, and often begged to be married, but her entreaties were to no avail. One day, as he was out on a business trip, her lover (whose name is not recorded) failed to return home, to Margaret's great distress. A few days later, when his dog returned without him, Margaret's worry grew even more. The dog pulled on her dress and led her through the woods to the place where the body of her lover lay, murdered.

This discovery horrified Margaret, not only for the physical sight of it, but because of what might have been the state of his soul upon his death. She recognized immediately that her fate could have been the same, and at the first opportunity, she gave away all the gifts and benefits she had gained as a mistress, and left Montepulciano with her son. She returned to her father's house, where her father and stepmother refused to welcome her. At this point, Margaret almost despaired of her situation, until she remembered the Franciscan friars at Cortona, and went to them.

She was received kindly by the friars, and began a new life of prayer, penance, and love of the great mercy of God. After a few years, she joined the Third Order of Saint Francis, and in addition to her life of prayer and penance, she took on a life of poverty, in imitation of Saint Francis. She began austere, penitential fasting practices, and subsisted only on alms. As her son grew older under the example of his holy mother, he later became a Franciscan friar himself. Eventually, she established a hospital for the sick and impoverished, and founded a congregation of Third Order Sisters called the "Poverelle" ("poor little women"). She also became involved in public affairs, once admonishing the Bishop of Arezzo for his behavior, which was unbecoming of a man of God.

After twenty-nine years in prayer and penance, Margaret died. The very day of her death, the people of Cortona declared her a

Saint, and began to build a church in her honor that same year. She was formally canonized by the Catholic Church in 1728.

Margaret was rejected by her stepmother, and then rejected by the townspeople of the town she had made her home. She was even rejected in some ways by her lover, in that she desired stability and legitimacy in her situation, but was denied it. Then, when her heart converted and she was ready to make amends, she was rejected by her family all over again. A reject, a pariah, an outcast. How often had I felt like an outcast in my life, too? I found in Saint Margaret a holy woman to whom I could relate, who knew what it was to be cast aside.

The thing about Saint Margaret, though, is that, for better or worse, she didn't wallow in it. When she was treated cruelly by her stepmother, she threw herself into recklessness, and eventually a life overtaken by sin. It's often so easy for us to do similarly. When the difficulties of life weigh heavy on us, we often cope in unhealthy or sinful ways. "It's not that bad," we tell ourselves. We convince ourselves it's something small that will help us manage the difficulty more easily, just this once. But eventually, we can find ourselves slipping further and further from the straight and narrow, from the path we know is better for us. We desensitize ourselves to the enormity of sin.

However, though Saint Margaret threw herself headlong into sin as a young woman, when she realized the horrors of the path she was on, she turned her whole soul to Christ and tenaciously persevered in clinging to Him. My own spiritual life has been punctuated by flashes in the pan; good-intentioned moments of extreme fervor that eventually fizzle out back to lukewarm mediocrity. Saint Margaret is an example of perseverance in our spiritual lives. She chose the better part, and wouldn't let it be taken away from her. That's not to say she didn't struggle, though. The first few years after her conversion, especially, were full of temptations to her old life. She knew that the luxuries and allurements of sin were more comfortable and pleasing than a life of prayer and penance. Surely, she must have wondered whether a return to her old life would have been more comfortable for her young son. But she was steadfast in her faith. She knew that nothing the world could offer her would ever be worth it, not for her or her son. She truly understood what it meant to find the "pearl of great price," and give away everything else to possess it.

Her life was characterized by "dysfunction," and mistakes aplenty. This is something that drew me to her. My entire life had been characterized by "dysfunction," too. In fact, my mom and I used to joke that we'd create a book series out of all our dysfunctional mishaps! I remember thinking to myself as I sat in the chapel of our convent one day, how strange is it for a woman with my "broken family" background to be in religious life? So many of the other Sisters came from seemingly perfect, large, devout families, and I often felt so out of place among them. But Saint Margaret's life comforted me. She had a son! Out of wedlock! And yet she became a famous penitent who not only established a hospital to care for the less fortunate, she founded a community of Sisters who would accomplish the work of the hospital and dedicate their lives to Christ, too. The Lord truly "lifts up the lowly," and as I saw it in Saint Margaret's life, I was able to see it in my own life, as well. Romans 8:28 became my favorite Bible verse, something that I frequently brought to my mind and continue to bring to my mind today: *"We know that all things work together for good for those who love God, who are called according to his purpose."* All things work together for good. No matter my mistakes, no matter my state in life, no matter my past, no matter anything I think can come between me and God, He can turn it around and make something glorious result from it.

"God writes straight with crooked lines," the saying goes, and if He could do it so beautifully in Margaret's life, He can surely do it in mine.

Eventually, I left the convent, after having been there for over five years. I was about three years away from making final vows. I wanted nothing more than to give my life completely to God, and at the time, I thought being in the convent was the best—or even only— way I could adequately do that. It became clear after the first year that I wasn't well-suited to the life, but I'm nothing if not stubborn, and so I stayed much longer than I should have. I spent many agonizing hours in prayer, asking God for the grace to know what to do. Should I stay and try harder? That didn't seem to be working. Should I leave? But what would people think? I'd be letting everyone down!

One day, I finally mustered up the courage to talk to our Mother Superior and ask to leave. It was one of the hardest decisions of my life, even more difficult than the decision to enter the convent. I left to go back home one sunny October morning, and though the trip home was joyful and I was strongly convicted that I was doing the right thing, it was still quite disorienting to go back to being a layperson "in the world" once again. A new life, starting from scratch, had begun, and though my heart was happy to know I was doing what God was asking of me and what was better for me, it was hard not to feel alone.

And so Saint Margaret of Cortona continued to be a beloved friend in Heaven. While she is often known solely as a penitent, a former sinner who turned her life around, she's even more to me than that. Although inspiring in the way she went from turning away from God for many years, to embracing a life dedicated to Him wholeheartedly, she's also a woman who understands what it's like to feel alone and outcast. When you find yourself feeling alone, you can always know you have an example and intercessor in Saint Margaret of Cortona.

If you ever feel despairing of the situation in your life, ask Saint Margaret for her intercession. She is a woman who experienced the crushing weight of desperate circumstances, most especially as a mother. Saint Margaret's story inspired me in new ways the moment I became a mother, and gave me a renewed appreciation for my own mother. Even as a child, I knew that being a single parent was difficult for her, but I never doubted her fierce love for my siblings and me, and I noticed the constant sacrifices she made for us, even though she never once complained about making them. This knowledge only grew deeper the older I got, and now as a mother myself, I am truly filled with awe at what my mother did for us, and I am forever grateful. No matter how difficult your circumstances, know that your children see and feel the deep love you have for them. Especially as they grow older and maybe someday become parents themselves, they will see even more clearly the depths of your love for them.

As a single mother during a time when such a thing was utterly scorned, Saint Margaret experienced the derision of those around her, and must have felt so much sorrow, not only for the scorn directed at her son, but also for the atmosphere in which her son would grow up. As mothers, we always want what is best for our children, and Saint Margaret was no exception. Eventually, however, once her heart converted back to Christ, she came to know that what is "best" isn't always what is more luxurious, or more comfortable, or easier. What is "best" is what is best for our souls, what leads our soul closer and closer to God. With this knowledge, she left her life of sin behind, including the comfort of a castle, and sought the "springs of living water, welling up to eternal life," (John 4:14) knowing that nothing could be better for her son than nourishing his spiritual life, and teaching him that "God so loved the world, that He gave His only begotten Son, that whoever believes in Him shall not perish, but have eternal life." (John 3:16)

Saint Margaret of Cortona remains an example to me of repentance, courage, charity, and perseverance in the spiritual life. In the Church seasons of fasting, I'm reminded how Saint Margaret fasted gladly, in a spirit of penance. In my difficult moments of parenting, I'm reminded how Saint Margaret endured some of the harshest conditions imaginable, and yet remained faithful to the Lord in such a way that her son became inspired to devote himself entirely to the Lord, too. When I'm overwhelmed and overburdened, I'm reminded of the charitable endeavors of Saint Margaret, how she dedicated her life, not only to prayer and penance, but to caring for the sick and less fortunate, and it inspires me to continue forward with my efforts, however meager, for the honor and glory of God. When I feel alone or cast away, I'm reminded of all the scorn that Saint Margaret endured, too. If Saint Margaret, by God's grace, can rise above all the difficulties of her life and become a great Saint, surely I can try, by God's grace, too. Saint Margaret of Cortona, pray to God for us!

REFLECTION QUESTIONS

1) People are made to connect to other people. We have a tendency to seek out community, and find solace there. When community is somehow missing from our lives, we can often feel the negative effects profoundly. Sometimes, despite our best efforts, a community seems impossible to find, or else if one exists, it can feel impossible to break through and be welcomed. Have you ever felt like an outcast? What are ways in which the Communion of Saints, and perhaps Saint Margaret of Cortona specifically, can help you feel like you're not alone or rejected?

2) As the saying goes, "God writes straight with crooked lines." No matter what paths our lives take, we know that God can turn things around for His honor and glory and the good of our souls.

From a young age, Saint Margaret made countless mistakes that eventually led to her living as a mistress and bearing a son. And yet, when she turned back to Christ, she became such a profound example of virtue and holiness that, on the day of her death, the people of Cortona unanimously declared her a Saint. What are some of the ways that my life has taken an unusual path to something good, particularly something that honored God?

3) Saint Margaret of Cortona had a son in unideal circumstances. When faced with the reality of her own mortality and the state of her soul, she turned wholeheartedly to Christ, and brought her son with her. In doing so, she gave away all the benefits she had gained during her old life: money, expensive clothing, and other such gifts that had been bestowed on her. It was incredibly difficult for her to do these things, but she knew it was necessary in order to follow Christ completely. When are times in my life that I've given up certain things in order to more closely follow Christ? Are there any ways I'm inadvertently clinging to something I know I should give up, in order to become more holy?

Opening Doors

SAINT MARIA OF PARIS
MARTYRED 1945 A.D.

Angela Doll

BEFORE I HAD CHILDREN of my own, I remember sitting in a restaurant with a friend and her seven-year-old. The child had chosen and ordered her meal and though my friend tried to talk her out of her choice, predicting that she wouldn't like what she'd chosen, her daughter could not be convinced. When the food came, she took one bite and complained that she didn't care for it. My friend happily switched plates with her, and that solved the problem without any further fuss. I remember, clearly, making a promise to myself that I'd never do that as a parent. I also remember making plans to never put away breakable things when I had children. I was certain I could teach them to handle things carefully. I had a great deal to learn. It turns out that those promises I made before I had children of my own, like fragile keepsakes around small baby hands, are made to be broken. It's remarkable to me how easy it is to make judgments without any real, tangible experience. The old adage about walking a mile in someone else's shoes really does hold up.

It is chilly this morning, and my office is uncarpeted. The slippers I chose thoughtfully a few months ago are on the giant feet of my youngest. His feet were cold, and though he did not ask, I gave him the fleece-lined shoes without a moment of hesitation. I recognize the feeling as it rises in me, seeing the need and then filling it. They are hungry, and I feed them. They are cold, and I find a way to make them warm. They are crying, and I comfort them. It's not that they are "spoiled," as I don't accept that term as it applies to humans. What do we do with things that are spoiled? No, my children are not spoiled; they have known pain, and cold, and hunger at times. I cannot always fill the need. They have not been shielded from difficulty. They have not been insulated from the world. Perhaps that is why I gave my youngest my shoes, precisely because he has been hurt. My youngest, in particular, has carried the hurt in his body. He has carried not only his own hurt, but often he has taken on the hurt of others as well, of his friends or his family who are struggling. He has been a kind of family "canary in a coal mine." So now I try to remedy the hurt. I try to take away the cold and the pain if I can. I want him to live. I want us all to live.

I entered into my marriage as a "child of divorce," a term that I have grown to hate with a passion. Growing up in the '70s and '80s, I was the only person I knew in my highly Catholic circles whose parents were divorced. I knew kids who had lost a parent, but none of them were lost to divorce. When my mother separated from my dad, our parish priest removed her from her layperson duties for a time. My mom spearheaded the guitar mass ministry in the 1970s at our parish, she was a lay communion distributor, worked with the school staff, and was active in every way. But back then, divorce was utterly stigmatized, no matter the circumstances.

Before he proposed, my ex-husband asked that I consent to the idea of a "no divorce" marriage. I was intrigued. I knew how my parents' divorce had affected me as a child, but more, I saw how it affected my mother. I didn't want to ever go through that, so I said "yes" without really knowing what door I was closing. I only saw that it forced me to figure things out if we had issues, and I thought that might be enough. As it turned out, the "figuring things out" part of the relationship was left to me most of the time, and I did that. I was good at it. I saw a need and I filled it. In fact, I rarely even looked at that closed door before me. Once we had our four children, there was no time to look at that door. It was boarded shut. It ceased to even be a door, just a memory of a door.

Mother Maria of Paris watches me as I write this. Her icon on my desktop, I can look past my laptop screen and meet her gaze. Her eyes are kind and a small smile plays at her lips, something I've seen in photographs of her. That smile is what drew me in the first time I saw those photographs. St Maria is a modern era saint. She lived and died before I was born, but not much before, in the scheme of things. She would have been a contemporary of my grandparents. Our life spans might have overlapped if she'd lived through World War II, perhaps.

Not long ago I read an article about old photos and videos being colorized, smoothed out, animated. They were made to match the moving images we are used to seeing every day on our televisions, our iPhones, our laptops. I watched a short clip of men, women, and children in New York City sometime around the 1940's throwing snowballs in the street. I watched it three times, marveling, thinking it was a trick of the industry. How can they look so recently living? It reminded me that these people were real, that they *are* real. I forget that sometimes when I look at icons. I forget that these saints are people who lived.

When I was 51 years old, I decided to leave my marriage. The discontent and unhappiness were brewing in me for a long time. I woke and prayed, unsure of why each morning brought a burning in my stomach, a rush of tears in the shower, a headache all day. I put on a brave face, though I went about my day in a kind of persistent low-level depression. No one even knew I was struggling. I knew, but I thought it was some shortcoming in me. I thought if I confessed my sin and just tried harder, I'd be okay eventually. I thought if I lost weight or learned more skills, got another degree, kept my house cleaner, counseled my children better, wrote more books, climbed higher in my career, then the knot at the pit of my stomach would dissolve. Then I went back to therapy, because I realized there were many things I said to myself that I never said out loud. They were terrifying things I could not admit to anyone, not even my priest. I needed to practice saying those things out loud to someone safe so that they would stop waking me in the middle of the night, stop tying knots in my stomach, stop feeding my depression and anxiety.

The last door that Mother Maria saw was that of the gas chamber. She was only a few years older when she died than I am now. Her life was not interrupted by war; she was shaped by it, and eventually, her life was taken by it. Each thread of the rich tapestry of her early life weaves a story of gift and grief, life and death. She was born in Russia on the shore of the Black Sea to parents who were devout in their Orthodox faith. Her father's death when she was fourteen shook her to her core. It is because she carried an inner compass of compassion tempered by a radical longing for justice that this loss of her father at such an age felt like injustice strong enough to shut the door to the existence of God. She became an atheist and pursued justice as the Bolshevik Revolution began. It was not an act of bitterness, but hope, a kind of revolution when no doors are open and knocking is no longer enough.

On my 25th wedding anniversary, I had a breakdown, or perhaps it was a revelation. I was reading *The Dark Night of the Soul* by St. John of the Cross and making the descent into my own dark night of the soul. My husband and I had no plans for our anniversary that night, so when he came to bed he said, "Happy 25th anniversary! Here's to another 25 years!" and I began to cry. I didn't want to live another 25 years the way we had been, but I had no idea how to articulate it yet. I was still only hearing whisperings of what was bothering me. I told him I was going to therapy. I asked if we could get back to couples therapy. His response was that he was busy with work and that "this was coming at a bad time" for him. The knot in my stomach growled and grew.

A few days later I had breakfast with a dear friend. Paula is a soul friend, someone with whom time has no bearing on our closeness. We drank coffee and ate cake in her kitchen after months apart, and it was as though no time had passed. We dove into conversations about her life and mine, her children and mine, her marriage and mine, and then I broke down crying. I told her that I was desperately unhappy and that I didn't know how to fix myself so that I could be happy again in my marriage. I told her that it felt as though I was locked in a room with a person I no longer loved and no longer even liked. The doors were locked; no matter how I knocked, I could not see an open door. I had no choice. My word is important to me. My vows were vital. I had chosen to agree to a "no divorce" marriage, and I was determined to survive that choice.

It was at that moment, possibly for the first time, that anyone suggested to me that marriage is not meant to be two people locked in a room together with no way out. She suggested that the doors of marriage should always be unlocked, because loving someone is a choice we need to make and one we ought to make every day with intention and care. That is how love grows and deepens. I felt like my heart broke open that day, and I left feeling hopeful for the first time. I thought this would fix me. I thought it would fix *us*. I wanted to find a way to open the doors again so that I could soften my heart and open it to my husband. My door was open. I saw a need and I filled it by trying to find a way through.

"I don't want a no-divorce marriage anymore," I told him. "I want us to choose each other. I want to have this door unlocked so we can grow." I was excited. I thought I had hit on the key to opening things back up for us. He was angry and said no. He said no to unlocked doors. He wanted them closed and locked, because without it, he said, he didn't trust that I would stay.

St. Maria was divorced twice. The first marriage ended as she began to open the door to her faith once again. Her husband left, and yet Christ was there for her. Her faith deepened as she worked to bring justice and beauty during times of revolution and then ultimately, the Second World War. When knocking on closed doors did nothing to stop the violence that continued to encroach, she found extraordinary strength, staying in Paris as food supplies were cut off, finding ways to feed the hungry and the poor, sheltering the homeless, providing baptismal certificates to spare those who would otherwise be taken away to concentration camps. She saw a need, and she filled it. She chose to stay when she was given the chance to leave, because while she wanted to live, she also wanted others to live.

I often read the lives of the saints, and I am comforted even as I am bothered. I compare myself, my circumstances, my trials, my responses, and I find myself failing. I wonder if Mother Maria felt like this. I wonder if she found herself failing? From the outside, I can make judgments about her. She stayed in her first marriage, but it was her husband who left, slamming the door behind him. She left her second marriage to open the door to follow Christ. There was a time when I would have judged her, the same way I did that day with my friend and her daughter. I would have anchored myself to that promise of a "no divorce" agreement, without really knowing at all what it would mean to live behind locked doors.

Here is what is miraculous, though. St. Maria of Paris did not create new doors to walk through, nor did she continue to simply knock and knock on closed doors in her life. She did not use violence to destroy. She did not find a key on the ground or pick the locks. St. Maria became a door, because this is the essence of what we do when we serve. When I give my son my shoes, I am becoming a doorway. When we comfort friends, when we feed the hungry, when we fight against injustice, when we listen to the marginalized, when we act to preserve life, and yes, even sometimes when we leave a marriage, we become a door to Christ.

This open door is what I see when I look into her eyes in photographs, in paintings, in the icon on my desk. She is real and present in those moments. I see the doorway to Christ, and I am comforted, I am sustained. I know without any doubt then that I am loved. I expect most who experienced her in life knew this when she became that doorway to Christ, that we are loved, and more than that, that we are worthy. Ultimately, this is what Christ tells us: we are loved and we are worthy of love. When we know that deeply and truly, we become able to convey that to others. I want to be that open door because I want to live. I want us all to live.

Reflection Questions

1) Jesus said, "I am the gate," in John 10. St. Maria became a door as she imitated Christ in serving others. In what way are you a door?

2) Motherhood means wanting us all to live. That desire draws on virtues of justice, bravery, moderation, self-control, wisdom, and love. What are your visceral feelings about motherhood and community? Have you given yourself and God credit for how motherhood thrives on virtue?

About the Authors

In Order of Their Chapters

Summer Kinard

Summer Kinard, who grew up spending happy days begging for stories and eloping in the woods, is an autistic author, publisher, and mother. She is the author of the ground-breaking book, *Of Such is the Kingdom: A Practical Theology of Disability* (Ancient Faith, 2019), a co-author of *Seven Holy Women: Conversations With Saints and Friends* (Ancient Faith, 2020), and editor and a contributing author of the highly-acclaimed devotional *Darkness is as Light* (Park End Books, 2020). She's the senior editor of the traditional small press, Park End Books (ParkEndBooks.com), the publishing home of the Accessible Church School curriculum project. Summer holds two master's degrees from Duke University Divinity School—an M.Div. (2003) and a Th.M. (2005, early church history and theology), and her lifelong love of the Bible and patristics inform her work as an autistic Orthodox Christian theologian. She and her husband Andrew, members of a parish in the Antiochian Diocese of Wichita and Mid-America, are rearing five autistic children of joy in Texas, with the help of their cheese-stealing poodle Doctor Horatio Biscuit. Follow her blog at SummerKinard.com.

CHARLOTTE RIGGLE

Charlotte Riggle is an Orthodox Christian whose love of stories of sanctity in lives with illness and disabilities carries throughout all of her work, whether in her day job in corporate accessibility or in her website articles and her children's books (*Catherine's Pascha* and *The St. Nicholas Day Snow*). She extends the hope of theosis for all people in her forthcoming book, *That God's Works Might Be Revealed: Lives of Disabled Saints* (Park End Books, 2023). Charlotte grew to love the Widow of Zarephath from hearing her story every Holy Saturday. She loves the way joy starts breaking out during that liturgy, like the first flowers of spring, with the buds on the trees all swollen, ready to explode with life, joy, and beauty. Even in her hardest times, there was the anticipation of joy. Always, in her time as a single mom, there was love, and with that, joy was there like the sun—you might not always be able to see it, but it would always be there. She wrote about the Widow of Zarephath to share her insights from getting older, her kids all grown, when she has time to look back, like Wordsworth said about the essence of poetry, with "emotions recollected in tranquility." The story of Elijah and the widow brings her to tears, but not tears of pain and frustration and sorrow, but tears that go with tranquility and joy.

SANDRA C. ANDERSON

Sandra Anderson is a nationally recognized leader in Orthodox Ministry Development. As the Ministry Coordinator at St. Mary's Greek Orthodox Church in Minneapolis for 17 years, she connected parishioners and the broader community to programs and ministries serving their needs, strengthening and promoting the faith, and engaging in fellowship. Through this position, which she helped to create, she worked with clergy through MEOCCA (Midwest Eastern Orthodox Christian Clergy Association), brought the Orthodox Prison Ministry program to Minnesota and expanded lay involvement in nonprofit ministries including Project Homeless Connect, Simpson House Shelter, FOCUS and more. Sandra has also done 20 years of ministry work at the Hogar Rafael Ayau in Guatemala. Her work with St. Mary's innovative summer camp, family camp and Koinonia programs, as well as her service as a Prepare/Enrich Counselor, have increased her exposure nationally. She is a sought after retreat leader who is preparing to share her experiences in her new book, A Handbook of Ministry Resources, Recommendations, and Reflections. Sandra's personal story, her passion for her faith, and her vibrant spirit resonate with so many who have been touched by her good works.

ELISSA BJELETICH DAVIS

Elissa Bjeletich Davis is an author and podcaster who loves Orthodox youth and family ministry work. She works on curriculum projects, teaches Sunday school, and volunteers at summer camps. For more than twenty years, Elissa was a married woman, whose work focused on creating Orthodox rhythms in the family. But when her own family fell apart, Elissa turned to St. Helena for comfort and inspiration, for company as she struggled with parenting her five children in an entirely new landscape. When the opportunity came to be a part of this collection, to open up and invite others into her journey with divorce and parenting alone, she couldn't possibly pass it up. She has avoided St. Helena, been inundated with St. Helena, and finally embraced and fallen in love with St. Helena, and it is such a joy to share that with you. Read more on in her blog post on this topic: https://blogs.ancientfaith.com/raisingsaints/new-book-the-grace-of-being-there/

Elizabeth Gatling

Elizabeth Gatling is a corporate research librarian and project manager by day/K-drama fan and fabulous cook by night, a cosplayer at cons, a faithful Orthodox Christian, and a builder of community and fun for herself, her son, and the many friends who love them.

K·RISTINA ROTH

Kristina Roth lives in the Black Hills of South Dakota with her spirited son and two scruffy dogs. She is a grant writer for a large nonprofit. Her essays, artwork, ghostwritten mental health content, and poems have been published in numerous anthologies, magazines, and websites. She is grateful for the astounding experience of motherhood and the creative and spiritual growth it can bring.

CARRIE CHUFF

Carrie Chuff is a wife and homeschooling mother of six children. As a young woman, she spent five years of formation in a Roman Catholic convent of active/contemplative religious Sisters whose apostolate included retreats and catechesis. After realizing God had other plans, she left and later met and married her husband, Derek. Eventually, they both rediscovered their Eastern Catholic heritage and embraced it fully as members of the Ukrainian Greek-Catholic Church, a Byzantine Rite Eastern Catholic Church which is in communion with Rome. She resides with her family in Hollidaysburg, Pennsylvania.

Angela Doll

Angela Doll is a poet, fiction writer, and essayist whose work has appeared or is forthcoming in *Thin Air Magazine, Apeiron Review, The Cresset, Eastern Iowa Review, St. Katherine Review, Rock and Sling, Elephant Journal, "Good Letters," Ruminate Magazine Blog,* and *Art House America.* Her memoir, *Nearly Orthodox: On Being a Modern Woman in an Ancient Tradition,* was published in 2014 by Ancient Faith Publishing, followed by, *Garden in the East* in 2016 and, *The Wilderness Journal* in 2018. Angela is the Managing Editor of *The St. Katherine Review,* where she delights in discovering and empowering new writers and established writers.

About the Illustrator

AND COVER ARTIST

MARY SARCHIZIAN

I am a dork and Orthodox misfit who is seeks God in places where people assume we can't find Him. I am inspired by iconography, graffiti, and anime. I make my art for people who have felt out of place in the Church or overlooked. For the outcasts, the misfits, and the people who God shows His glory through in unsuspecting ways. I want people to see the saints as an example and a refuge, no matter who they are or what they face in life. I illustrated this book because I wanted to be a part of making the Church more aware of the holy and loving work that single mothers do, and that we have many beautiful examples among the saints. I want people to see themselves and their struggles in the saints, instead of just untouchable heroes adorned in gold leaf.

About Park End Books

PARK END BOOKS

Park End books brings beautiful, accessible Orthodox and Catholic books to the mainstream market.

COMING SOON:

HOSPITALITY FOR HEALING
By Melissa Naasko

Care for the sick with wisdom and proven recipes based on convalescent cookbooks and the traditions of monastic infirmaries.

Seasoned with the warmth and wisdom she experienced in her abuela's kitchen, Matushka Melissa Naasko brings together the healing traditions of early 20th Century convalescent cookbooks and the long tradition of healing customs in monastic infirmaries. With the practicality readers have come to expect from her popular cookbook *Fasting as a Family* and her workshops, Mat. Melissa highlights what it means to help others recuperate in a time when new and chronic illnesses are more common than ever.

OTHER TITLES TO CONSIDER FROM PARK END BOOKS

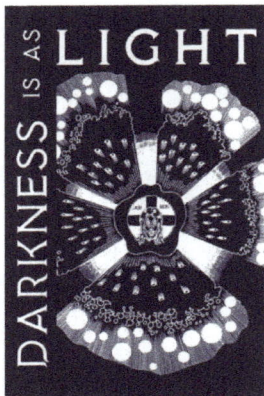

DARKNESS IS AS LIGHT:
CHRISTIAN WOMEN'S DEVOTIONS FOR PERSISTING
IN HARD PLACES
By Twenty-Two Orthodox, Catholic, and Saint-Loving
Christian Women; Edited by Summer Kinard

"Each entry sings with one theme: Christ is present. And it is this present God we can trust to sustain us, draw us closer, and sanctify us, no matter what." -*Sojourners Magazine*

In the beautifully illustrated and highly acclaimed devotional Darkness is as Light, twenty-two Christian women bear witness in order to help readers see God with them in suffering, recognize hope in the hardest of experiences, and learn to reach sideways in the darkness to those companions who are alongside them in their struggles.

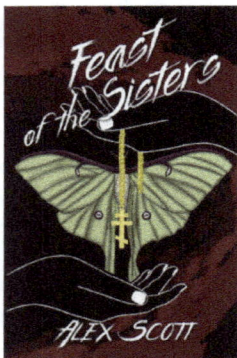

FEAST OF THE SISTERS
By Alex Scott

"This young adult vampire novel kept me on the edge of my seat." -April Marie, reader

When Vicki disappears, gentle and sensitive Jo vows to do whatever it takes to save her-even tracking Vicki through the haunted lair and secret tunnels of a notorious, immortal killer. Will Jo and her friends stop the feast before it happens, or will they become its guests of honor?

www.ingramcontent.com/pod-product-compliance
Lightning Source LLC
Chambersburg PA
CBHW070333090426
42733CB00012B/2468